MEDITATION   K

Meditation is
not only an activity that
is easily performed, but it is also
within anyone's reach, regardless of their
lifestyle or religious or philosophical persuasion.
Another widely held belief is that meditation's only goal
is spiritual enlightenment, such as was attained by the
Buddha. Without excluding the possibility of transcendence, the practice of meditation results
almost immediately in enhanced creativity
and learning ability, as well as the
elimination of physical
tension and stress.

MEDITATION GUIDEBOOK

JOSÉ LORENZO-FUENTES

Translated by

ANTONIO PALOMO

Smriti Books
New Delhi (INDIA)

ISBN: 81-87967-67-6

First Indian Edition: Delhi, 2004

(Reprinted from *Meditation: Practice and Application*,
published by Llewellyn Publications, USA)

Publishers
SMRITI BOOKS
Email: smritibooks@vsnl.net
Website: www.sphenterprises.com

Distributors
NEW AGE BOOKS
A-44 Naraina Phase I
New Delhi-110 028 (INDIA)
Email: nab@vsnl.in
Website: www.newagebooksindia.com

For Sale in Indian Subcontinent Only

Printed in India
by Jainendra Prakash Jain at Shri Jainendra Press
A-45 Naraina Phase-I New Delhi-110 028 (INDIA)

To Lida,
a guardian angel
who inspired this book

My thanks to Mercy Palomo, Belkis Cuza Malé,
Nilda Tejedor, Alejandro Ramírez, Danny Lorenzo,
Tony Palomo, Nila Danza, Bárbara Pernaris,
and my daughter Gloria Lorenzo
for their support in drafting this book.

Contents

Introduction   xi

Part I: The Repair System   1
Results of Meditation. Breathing Rhythm. Thermic
Alternation Breathing. Meditation Breathing. Breathing
In and Out. Breathing Infinity.

Part II: The Art of Meditation   15
Back straight. Eyes half-closed. Hands on your lap. Tongue
against your palate. Reasons to meditate. The Meditator's
Ten Commandments. Karma and health. Astral projections.
Directed meditations. How to shape your future. How to
fight fear.

Part III: Buddhist Meditation   41
Satori. Psychic powers. Extrasensory perceptions. Intuition.
The answers of the Old Man. Intuition and the New Age.
The Twelve New Words.

Part IV: The Warrior's Rest   57
How to master stress. Learning to relax. And now, start to
meditate. Return to the womb. Sun and surf. A special place.

Part V: Health and Longevity   71
Mental alchemy. Cellullar intelligence. Chromotherapy and
meditation. The skylight. Origin of disease. Risotherapy
(Laughter Therapy). Reviving mirth. Healing through the
Five Elements. How to heal at a distance. Learning to
close up.

Part VI: The House of Health   **93**

Taking advantage of the biorhythm. Healing meditation.
Tantric self-healing. The Master Healer. The power to heal.
Psi Healing. The Sphere of Energy. Healing and Cosmic
Consciousness. Healing hands. Self-healing exercises.
Exercise 1. Exercise 2. Exercise 3. Exercise 4.

Part VII: Zen and Self-Realization   **109**

Mind control. Any technique is the best. The face of God.
Self-actualization and success. Love, astrology, and meditation. How to awaken latent abilities. How to materialize
money.

Part VIII: Seven Healing Meditations   **129**

Bibliography   137

Introduction

We have heard or known about Buddhism in the West for a very, very long time, but it was only in 1826 that the first study on Buddhism was published in France by Lasen and Burnouf. However, Buddhism really made its debut in 1875, the year Helena Petrovna Blavatsky and Colonel Henry Steel Olcott founded the Theosophical Society, whose goal, among others, was to encourage the comparative study of religions, philosophies, and sciences.

Annie Besant, Blavatsky's successor as worldwide leader of Theosophy, undertook a remarkable effort to spread Hinduism and Buddhist teachings in the West, thus paving the way for many Zen masters, such as Hakuun Yasutani, who lived for some time in the US lecturing on the Buddhist dharma. Thus Buddha's own prediction started to come true, as mentioned in the text addressed to Vimaladevi, titled *Prophesy*: "Twenty five hundred years after my final nirvana, the true doctrine shall be spread in the land of the red-faced," a clear allusion to the spread of Buddhism in the United States.

A new impetus took place when the priest Enomiya Lasalle finally built the Akikawa-Shinmeikutsu Center, located in the vicinities of Tokyo, devoted to spreading the teaching and practices of Buddhism.

When the Buddhist lamas, victims of political persecution, were forced to abandon Tibet and sought refuge in many other countries, they devoted themselves to preaching and disseminating their doctrine in the lands that took them.

Finally, it is the spiritual phenomenon known as the New Age movement that has completed the expansion of Buddhism in the West and, therefore, has given rise to the worldwide boom experienced by the practice of meditation.

Part I
The Repair System

People's welfare relies on
their ability to return to nature.

—**Lao Tzu**

Nothing is more remarkable
about the human body
than its recuperative drive.

—**Norman Cousins**

According to the Zohar, Wisdom (the Male Principle) and Intelligence (the Female Principle) joined to give birth to a child similar to both its father and its mother—Knowledge. Therefore, any attitude toward life is wrong if it is not based on Knowledge, the providential offspring of Wisdom and Intelligence.

If we were to establish a list of priorities, the first knowledge we most urgently would have to acquire is the most difficult knowledge of all—knowledge of oneself. There is a silent zone in the deepest layer of our being that people instinctively refuse to contact because it is more pleasant for them to venture outside of it in search of all kinds of satisfaction. Thus they create for themselves the first illusion, which immediately makes them dependent on anything they are able to see, taste, touch, measure, and appreciate through their physical senses. Holding fast on to the claims made by the outer world with the strength of all our instinctive forces, seeking protection and safety, is paradoxically the quickest way we can substantiate the condition of helplessness to which we are doomed. Like Prometheus, we remain fettered to a rock while the passions, the unsatisfied wishes, the boundless ambitions, and the frustrations devour our entrails. Without expectations there can be no life—that much is true. Without actions and the fruit of those actions it would not be possible to accumulate experiences in order to acquire wisdom—just as expectations, ambition, and actions lack an adequate course to develop harmoniously if we haven't previously reconciled acts and aspirations with our inner being, with the intelligence that inhabits the molecular structure of our body.

One of the many purposes of meditation is to awaken us to self-knowledge, to teach us to listen to the music of our body, its rhythms and messages, its most intimate calls. If someone manages to stop in his or her tracks, sits down comfortably and dedicates him- or herself to listening to the information that his or her body is constantly transmitting, he or she will acquire without effort the necessary knowledge to attain wisdom, which is ultimately nothing but the enjoyment of all the perceptions of love, compassion, happiness, and well-being afforded to us by the Universe.

Until a few years ago, for most people the practice of meditation belonged exclusively to the field of mysticism and was basically associated with the development of psychic awareness and paranormal faculties. Even though it is true that during meditation innumerable paranormal phenomena can and often do happen, among them communicating with extraterrestrial beings or with people already deceased, that is not precisely the aspect that arouses most interest today—but rather it is its attributes related to improving our health. Sure enough, thousands and thousands of physicians throughout the world are learning to meditate or have devoted years to its practice because they were able to see for themselves the beneficial physiological results that take place in a person as soon as he or she starts to meditate. The heart rate slows down while blood pressure simultaneously drops, and metabolic activity, usually measured by the amount of oxygen used up by the body, decreases to levels much lower than during prolonged and restful sleep. But there's still a lot more. Research conducted at Harvard, Stanford, Yale, and other major universities has shown that meditation is not only effective in lowering blood pressure and cholesterol levels while strengthening the immune system, but also in fighting all kinds of illnesses, including a disease as aggressive as cancer.

"Cancer patients can survive longer if they are trained in techniques such as relaxation and hypnosis," asserted F. Fawzy, M.D., psychiatry professor at the University of California in Los Angeles, in his report published in *Archives of General Psychiatry*, in which he set forth the broadest compilation of scientific research to this date. We add that they not only can survive longer, but also even achieve a cure. It is already known that numerous people have been able to conquer disease when they appealed to the great reserves of their imagination to get their organism's defense system going, just like guided imagery therapies seem to be an important factor in the remission of many cancers.

The prestigious physician Andrew Weil, M.D., a Harvard graduate and for many years Director of the Department of Social Medicine of Tucson University in Arizona, in his book *Spontaneous Healing* (Ballantine, 2000), dealt at length with the human body's ability to repair itself while maintaining health and preventing diseases. That's the same opinion expressed by many scientists who no longer refer to a central nervous system, an endocrine system, and an immune system, but rather to a single recovery system that, as Bernie Siegel said, comprises a kind of super intelligence that dwells inside of us (*Love, Medicine and Miracles*, Harper & Row, 1986).

Everything seems to indicate that disease arises when we don't live according to our inner intelligence, when we don't respect the natural laws that, as proclaimed in ancient Greece, guaranteed a healthy mind in a healthy body. In short—when we are not able to activate our repair system.

To reach and maintain the level of health we desire, the first thing we have to do is believe in the possibility that the super intelligence that Siegel talked about can be activated by our thoughts.

No one can live without believing in something, but only those who possess a system of beliefs whose foundations are compassion, love, happiness, and altruism can live healthily. To believe is to keep an expectation alive. That is why it has been said that the most frequent disease of the elderly is experience, because living all those long years almost always weakens their belief system through the loss of expectations. They cease to believe in the possibility of conquering a new love, of someone else needing their protection or of being able to lend a helping hand—they stop believing in other people and end up ceasing to believe in themselves, which is the same as forgetting and neglecting that inner intelligence that could otherwise still work for a long time to foster their health.

An ancient Greek story, re-created by Jorge Luis Borges in one of his most fascinating literary works, tells of a king that died of hunger and thirst in the midst of fountains and gardens. Logic tells us that this could not happen in real life. No one can die of thirst if water is within reach, or starve to death in the middle of a garden, which is also supposed to have fruit-bearing trees. The anecdote, of course, has a symbolic value: it instills the notion that we can lose our health and even our lives if we are not aware of the infinite resources that are available to us to prevent death and disease.

When we face any situation, we usually employ our common sense to infer whether the result of our actions is going to be positive or negative. There are always two possibilities: success or failure. These two possibilities are set in the future, so both of these options, since neither has been actualized, belong to the field of the imagination. We can imagine that everything will go well or, on the contrary, that our efforts won't yield the result we're after. Neither of the two possibilities has yet manifested itself on the physical plane, but tomorrow (that is, at any time) one of these two options will reach the plane of reality. Success or failure will become real. Then, if we become aware that up to that moment the obstacle or failure was imaginary, it is only truly reasonable to deny failure the ability to dwell in our minds, forget that option exists, and think that success will crown our efforts.

Ernest Hemingway used to say that he wrote his novels and short stories with greater skill when he was in love. That confession amounted to acknowledging that his creative capacity grew when a strong motivation appeared in his life, that is, when his ego was nourished by a pleasant emotion that filled him with enthusiasm and the ardent desire to enjoy life to its fullest. On another occasion Hemingway said that he wrote better when he was in good health. Instinctively the great writer used two keywords: health and love. So we go back to the same issue: without love, without happiness, without enthusiasm, without the pleasant need to communicate with our mate or with another person, and ideally with many other people, and with all living things, if we are not able to give our love to plants and animals, if we are not thrilled by a sunset—it is not possible to reach perfect health.

We should emphasize the following statement: when nothing awakens pleasant emotions, if we don't beam love and happiness to others, that is when disease will appear. When a person feels unable to solve his or her problems, whatever those problems might be, when that person is overwhelmed by anguish or fear, when that person thinks those problems are insurmountable, then that person decides to flagellate him- or herself and gets sick. Perhaps "decide" is not the most suitable word, since the only option that person discovered (disease), was not chosen consciously. It is known that heart attacks are more frequent on Monday mornings than on any other day of the week. That's when the working week starts, and without a doubt the only explanation possible is that people who hate their work escape from it by bringing a heart attack on themselves. It has also been shown that heart disease may be the result of lack of love in any of its manifestations, that deep resentment can give rise to cancer, and that asthmatics are usually people who seek reassurance from other people at all costs. In her book *Imagery in Healing: Shamanism and Modern Medicine* (Shambhala, 2002), Jeanne Achterberg mentions the influence exerted by images on our physiological processes such as heart rate, blood glucose levels, bowel activity, and breathing. A host of alterations take place in our bodies, for better or for worse, as soon as a person visualizes a certain situation in a positive or negative manner. If that is evident, if even science is paying ever-growing attention to the mind-body relationship, perhaps we ought to ask ourselves whether we should reassess our attitude toward life right now. Of course we should. We need to reassess our attitude in order to mobilize our inexhaustible reserves of energy to actualize to the utmost, the sooner the better, our creative potential. To do so today would be better than doing so tomorrow.

Just as King Midas turned everything he touched into gold, we can go our merry way, if we truly want to, turning everything around us into what we have imagined it should be, so powerful are our inner forces. When the eminent psychologist Carl Jung asserted that the future is as real as a thief, he was referring specifically to the human faculty to shape our own destiny through imagination. Our remotest forebears were not ignorant of the fact that they were able to harness the powers of the mind to transform objective reality or to create new situations. When primitive men painted an animal smitten with arrows in the caves of Altamira, they performed an act of magic to ensure the success of the hunt. That is why it's been said that in cave paintings we find the origins of visualization, the technique used by an ever- growing number of people to shape their future, create their short- or long-term goals, a technique that was also used by the ancient Greek healers, among them Aesculapius, Galen, and Hypocrites, who was the first to point out that what affects the mind harms the body.

Imagining means simply mobilizing our internal energies toward reaching a certain goal. When Taoists talked about "chi" energy, or when Hindu philosophers pointed out that all physical appearance is an illusion, traditional science replied that such assertions could only be made in the field of mysticism, since up until that time it had been apparently proven that everything real was material. However, ever since physicists started to explore the properties of the atom, a series of discoveries ensued that changed our view of the world. Einstein's famous equation, $E = mc^2$ (energy equals mass times the speed of light squared) taught us that mass and energy are manifestations of one single property. Thanks to the contributions made by quantum physics we can now assert that matter is energy at such a low rate of vibration that is becomes visible to the naked eye. Or, put another way, that energy can condense until it forms a *thing*, that is, any object whatsoever such as a chair, a table, a building, et cetera. If this is acceptable from the standpoint of modern physics—why are we going to doubt that any of us, by using our imagination, by visualizing an object, will be able to condense enough energy to transform that image into a material object?

This new conviction leads us to ask ourselves another question: why not utilize the mechanism through which imagination can be harnessed to our advantage, and make our wishes come true? It is already known that this mechanism that leads both to individual health and personal success can be activated by relaxation exercises, meditation, visualization, prayer, and hypnosis. Dr. Herbert Benson of Harvard Medical School's Mind/Body Institute said that his office received numerous calls every week from HMOs (health maintenance organizations) interested in the medical use of relaxation and other nontraditional therapeutic approaches. "If these healing methods are effective and can be employed reliably," remarked Dr. Benson. "They will not only be extremely useful to the patient but also to health organizations, which by using them will find they can reduce their health care costs."

Almost at the same time an independent panel convened by the National Institute of Health came to the conclusion that integrating relaxation therapy with conventional medical treatment is indispensable in order to fight many diseases successfully, and that, for example, relaxation methods can "lower the respiration and heart rates as well as blood pressure." The panel added it would not recommend any specific behavioral technique, but it emphasized that any of them could work, provided it included the "focus on one repetitive word, sound, sentence, phrase, or muscle activity."

Using these relaxation techniques is a must nowadays. Technology has enabled a good portion of the human race to reach an unprecedented level of physical comfort, but it has not been able to help man achieve personal actualization, and quite the opposite, seems to be the direct cause of his mental and emotional deterioration. There is a sense of dissatisfaction caused by reckless technological development, both in extremely poor countries and in developed and developing nations. Material abundance has only managed to increase anguish, frustration, lack of faith in the future, and therefore the pressing need to use tranquilizers, drugs, cigarettes, and alcohol. This overwhelming burden placed on modern man has come to be known as stress, a name used in medicine to identify the deterioration caused in the body by the constant changes resulting from technological development. Human beings cannot adapt to these changes at the same rate required by spiraling material progress. It is this inability, from which no one is exempt, that is soon reflected at a physiological and biochemical level. More than half the deaths in highly developed countries are due to heart disease, which, as everyone knows, have been caused by stress. Since, based on the foregoing, it is impossible to change the rules of the game for the time being, and, no matter how much we wish for it, stress cannot be suppressed, individuals must learn to master stress by increasing their bodily resistance to the tension generated by modern life.

Of all the relaxation techniques, the most effective way to achieve this purpose is through meditation. When a person starts to meditate regularly, that person reaches a deep sense of peace and restfulness that unquestionably soon produces an improvement in bodily health, in emotional stability, and therefore in the performance of his or her activities. Not only is meditation the ideal technique to face stress and relieve the tensions that are the cause of so many diseases, but also the ideal technique to unleash human potential by releasing the inexhaustible reserves of energy and creativity that we need in order to respond to the challenges imposed by our society's growing technological development.

From the viewpoint of oriental medicine, illness appears when, for any reason, a person loses his or her inner harmony, so any treatment must be focused on directing the patient's streams of life energy back to the course where they used to flow, thus gaining back that person's health and well-being. Of course this is not as easy as we have briefly stated because it not only involves the restoration of inner balance, but also enables the life force to flow again without interruption in the powerful stream of universal energy. A sick person is a one who somehow has decided to isolate him- or herself, who has interrupted his or her exchange of information with cosmic intelligence. Biologically, the body is programmed to repair itself. To recover equilibrium it is only necessary to awaken the organism's healing response.

That is not only achieved by using the technological means of conventional medicine. Good medical practice requires, in addition, all the wisdom of religion and all the techniques of magic, as Andrew Weil, M.D., has emphasized. Without wisdom or magic it does not seem possible to rouse the capacity for self-healing that dwells in every life form and most particularly in human beings. That is one of the many objectives sought by the practice of meditation: to promote spontaneous healing and activate the body's repair system.

An ever-growing number of people sit comfortably every day on a chair or couch and start to meditate. They have chosen a technique that does not take much effort and soon affords them a pleasant state of relaxation. Immediately thereafter meditators will experience, perhaps for the first time, the strange sensation of traveling into their own selves, encountering unsuspected levels of awareness that allow them to finally get to know themselves and (why not?) to reach the coveted *samadhi*, the state of supreme peace and well-being where we are one with the All and where nothing is felt or perceived.

Results of Meditation

"Meditating is easy, but preparing for meditation is very difficult," said Swami Sivananda. We'll deal more at length with the preparatory aspects of the practice of meditation later on. Now we only wish to emphasize that, against generally held belief, meditating is not only an activity that is easily performed but that is also within anyone's reach, regardless of that person's lifestyle or religious or philosophical persuasion.

Another widely held belief is that meditation's only goal is spiritual enlightenment, such as was attained by the Buddha. Without excluding the possibility to transcend, and therefore to reach higher states of consciousness, the practice of meditation provides the following results almost immediately:

- Elimination of tensions accumulated in the body.
- Drop in blood pressure.
- Elimination of stress.
- Enhanced learning ability.
- Enhanced creative capacity.

Western scientists who became interested in meditation have performed and published numerous experiments showing that as soon as a person starts to meditate his or her psycho-physiological connection is strengthened, resulting in improved health. This improvement soon becomes obvious in a noticeable drop in blood pressure and blood cholesterol levels. In many countries experiments have been performed to measure the brain waves of Buddhist monks in meditation, confirming that in the course of the practice of meditation the monks' alpha-waves measured 8 to 13 Hertz, thus enabling them to reach a state of total relaxation, which seems to be the secret for bodily health. Recent studies have shown that long-experienced meditators are able to not only stop the aging process but reverse it, resulting in a biological age that is impressively younger than their chronological age. Thanks to this research we also know that stress and worrying weaken the immune system and speed up the aging process, which is nothing but the progressive deterioration of our body's functions. Thus it is easy to infer that by reducing stress our capacity to live many years without the scourge of disease is enhanced, thereby accepting the so-called "senior years" as a happy life stage to be enjoyed.

Breathing Rhythm

Breathing has a natural rhythm, as does everything else in the Universe: the rhythm of seasons, of tides, and the rotation of the earth around its axis, giving rise to days and nights. But this rhythm, according to the advice of the yogis, must be "tamed gently and with persistence." Physiology teaches us that the function of the pituitary, the gland located close to the nasal cavity, is intimately involved with the inner clockwork whose rhythm controls the developmental stages of everyone: childhood, adolescence, old age, et cetera. But yogi doctrine emphasizes that pituitary rhythms are controlled by the breathing rhythm, and therefore if we learn how to master this rhythm we'll be able to slow down the aging process, thereby noticeably prolonging our useful years.

Taoist teachings classify breathing into three categories:

1. **Wind.** This breathing involves the natural function of the respiratory system: the "wind" is the air, which is essential to preserve life.

2. **Chi.** By breathing the body accumulates energy and by the practice of meditation respiration becomes more peaceful and slower.

3. **Hsi.** By persisting on the practice of meditation respiration becomes so slow that it gives the impression of having stopped while a breathing rhythm based in the lower abdomen comes to prevail. This is the breathing known as *Hsi.*

In order to master the breathing rhythm, which is so important for the person who decides to meditate, we recommend several exercises that will release the tensions accumulated in the body as a first measure to fight stress.

Thermic Alternation Breathing

Sit comfortably. Place the right hand's index and middle fingers between the eyebrows. With the thumb close off the right nostril and breathe in through the left nostril while counting up to eight. Now close the left nostril with the ring finger and breathe out through the right nostril, also counting to eight. Next breathe in through the right nostril and breathe out through the left one. Then do it in reverse.

The regular performance of this exercise will enable you to perceive the breathing rhythm's thermic alternation: the air that enters through one nostril is cold and exits through the other nostril hot. This exercise, in time, also creates an awareness of vital energy, enabling us to visualize that energy and take it to any part of the body that we want to revitalize.

Meditation Breathing

One of the respiratory exercises that yields the best results is the one called "full breathing," which is a totally abdominal or diaphragmatic breathing, also known as "meditation breathing."

It must be performed in a fully restful state, lying on one's back and with arms extended to the side. Breathe in slowly through the nose until filling up the lower portion of the lungs while the abdomen rises.

Once you finish breathing in you start breathing out, also through the nose, with your mouth closed, until you can press your belly.

"Full breathing" may be performed several times on the same day, provided it does not cause fatigue.

Here's another exercise that we most emphatically recommend:

Sit comfortably on a cushion, keeping your back straight.

Put together the soles of your feet.

Tilt your head slightly forward.

Put together the thumb and middle finger in each hand.

Now concentrate on the rhythm of your breathing.

When breathing in imagine you are storing the purest energy in the Universe inside.

Visualize that energy flowing throughout your body. You may visualize it as a beam of light or as liquid crystal penetrating all your organs.

When you finish the exercise, repeat mentally or aloud any mantra. If you don't remember any, repeat the word Om, prolonging as much as possible the letter *m*.

Breathing In and Out

When breathing in be conscious that you're breathing in, and when breathing out be conscious that you're breathing out.

Meditation Posture

A moment later you should put all your attention on the pauses that take place between breathing in and breathing out. They are very brief time spans, but it is very important that you be aware of them because these pauses will serve as your guidepost on your journey to your inner self, which is one of the main goals of meditation.

Now put all your attention on the sensation caused by the air as it comes in and out of your nostrils. Imagine that the air coming in brings you vitality while the air coming out carries to the outside world all the negativity accumulated in your body.

Breathing Infinity

Lie down on your back in an open area.

Gaze into the sky while you relax your body and start to become aware of your breathing rhythm.

Imagine that the air breathed in reaches your nostrils from the heavens, beyond the clouds.

Now you are breathing the air contained in infinity. In spite of the distance that supposedly separates you from the infinite, by breathing you and infinity are one and the same.

Not a single thought comes to your mind, or a single concern. Feel happy and actualized. You are breathing infinity.

Breathe it in for as long as possible.

Part II

The Art of Meditation

*The spiritual healing that takes place
with meditation is at least as
important as the physiological benefits.*

—Bernie Siegel

The first thing a meditation candidate learns is that there are different ways to practice meditation. There is, for example, the meditation that emphasizes repeating a sound, and the meditation that teaches mainly to concentrate on the breathing rhythm. One of the techniques that has gathered the largest number of devotees is transcendental meditation, introduced in the West by Maharishi Mahesh Yogi in the late fifties. Transcendental meditation teaches that the repetition of a sound is a powerful tool to reduce mental activity so that the mind's attention is turned inward, as if we attempted to dive in search of ever-more peaceful levels of awareness in the depths of ourselves.

The sounds used in transcendental meditation are called *mantras*. Mantra is a Sanskrit word meaning "prayer." It can also be translated as "a thought whose effects are known." Hence for Westerners a mantra is a phrase that is repeated to achieve a certain goal. Hindus refer to the repetition of a mantra as *japa* and compare it to the effort made by a person trying to awaken another person by shaking him or her. If we understand the symbolism of this comparison, we'll realize immediately that awakening a person is equivalent to returning that person to life, to giving life to that person. That is the function of the mantra—to unleash by sound the creative power of the mind. "Whenever mentally and vocally pronounced with creative force, the natural name of anything will give life to the thing that bears that name," said Arthur Avalon, one of the great interpreters of India's religiosity. According to this point of view, the creative power of the mind "travels" in sound to make possible a magic act thanks to which the individual makes his or her wishes come true. Humanity, which is a God on a lesser scale, thus successfully imitates the fascinating magic employed by the Creator, who said: "Let there be light." And there was light.

The practice of meditation enables us to make contact with our true inner nature, of whose knowledge and enjoyment we've been robbed by the whirl of uncontrollable emotions and activities imposed by the ever-accelerating rhythm of our modern world. Dazzled by this encounter with our own selves, we realize not only that in our own interior there lived a guest practically unknown to us but something even more important: that we will never be able again to part with his or her company.

When we meditate and leave behind thoughts dealing with our conscious activities, while we aim at the depths of our mind, we also experience the unshakable sensation that as of that very moment we will never be the same again. Indeed, meditating is almost like reaching a state of resurrection, at least grasping a new meaning of life, of an existence filled with more joy and creative possibilities. And as we continue to descend we realize that the frustrations, anger, and fear, which until then had been able to find abode in our hearts, are also being left behind—ever more so each time.

Everything that was cloudy becomes crystal-clear, and as we go through unknown regions that appear to be successive layers of liquid glass, we draw near, without hurry or effort, to a gratifying splendor that in reaching its end lets us know we are about to attain the purest light. Feeling wrapped by the light, a light that gets into every pore, and accepting the idea that we have turned into light, these are always new experiences that coincide with the ultimate purpose of meditation: enlightenment—just as reached by Buddha while sitting on a grass cushion under the asvattha tree, a ficus, which for Hindus is a symbol of the Universe.

In mentioning the introspective process of the meditator, which makes it possible to cross various levels of consciousness until reaching the very bottom of biological life, we have done nothing but refer directly to the origin of mysticism.

All mystics, from Saint Augustine to Sor Juana Inés de la Cruz, attained ecstasy by knocking on meditation's door and entering the interior of that enclosure where at last they were able to cast off, as a heavy and cumbersome burden, their worldly concerns, and then enter the kingdom of happiness.

This is why we find it curious that modern man, whose brain is forced to perform excessive cortical activity, which without a doubt causes irreversible damage to his central nervous system, has turned his back for years and years to therapeutic practices whose purpose it is to prevent the loss of inner harmony, whose lore has been compiled by humankind since the dawn of civilization. This also explains why in the past few decades there has been an increasing interest in alternative medicine and therapeutic practices such as hypnosis, acupuncture, and meditation. Many people who live in developed countries have stated that they are willing to pay a health insurance supplement that would cover some form of alternative medicine.

Seeking to remedy this deficiency in modern individuals, who hardly have any time left to turn their eyes inside themselves, Dr. Patricia Carrington of Princeton University put together a so-called "clinically standardized meditation." It is a new alternative leaning toward synthesis, a compendium that preserves the essence of all the ancient variations of the art of meditation, and an initiative that should make us all rejoice. Dr. Carrington designed this new alternative to allow people, after a hard day's work, to reconcile themselves with their inner selves. Her ability to develop this new modality is due to the fact that there exist indispensable features that endow any form of meditation with a touch of authenticity: the back upright, the eyes half-closed, the tip of the tongue turned to the palate and hands on one's lap.

Back Straight

When asked about Zen meditation in a sitting position, Zen Master Bankei replied: "Simply closing one's eyes and sitting down is not what I call meditation. Only meditation in a sitting position in harmony with subtle knowledge should be considered valuable. Meditating in a sitting position with subtle knowledge is the highest practice."

Sitting seems to be the golden rule in the art of meditating. The Bhagavad Gita already prescribed these rules for meditation: "In a purified location place a firm seat, covered with wool and deer skin, and, on top of the mat, kusa grass." But the Bhagavad Gita immediately underscored that the right posture was not just any sitting position but rather it must be performed "with the trunk, neck, and head firm and in a straight line."

All the ancient yoga texts recommend that meditation be performed with a straight back, ideally in the lotus position, that is, with one's feet crossed, the right foot over the left thigh, and the left foot over the right thigh. Since most Westerners don't find it easy to assume this posture, they are asked at least to keep their back upright while they meditate.

The first anatomic structure form in the fetus in the spine. That may be why it later becomes the support of the entire body, the canal through which all the wiring of the nervous system goes, and the receptacle of kundalini energy. Keeping our back straight while meditating means that we acknowledge the importance of the spine in our psychosomatic makeup and at the same time the role it plays in the breathing rhythm, which we cannot disregard when we start our journey to our inner world.

There isn't the slightest doubt that when we meditate with our back straight we breathe better. Thanks to breathing, the vital force enters the body, so a bent back hinders the breathing rhythm and undermines the organism's vitality. When a person adopts this posture, it seems as if he or she is refusing to breathe and therefore to accept life. Meditating with our back straight prevents compressing the abdominal organs and quiets down the heart and lungs. And if we manage to calm our heart, to reduce or spread the heartbeats, according to the yogi's theory we'll be able to prolong life. In yoga the duration of life is given by the number of breaths we take. That is why there is the need to practice slow, deep breathing as much as possible.

The theory of yoga teaches that through a series of breathing exercises one reaches the meditative state of muscle relaxation and therefore of control of physiological functions. According to yoga, the air holds two fluids: one, which we call oxygen, and another which yogis call *prana*, which is precisely the vital force, without which health would be impossible.

Prana, according to this theory, contains in turn two fluids: one male or solar called *Pingala*, which the Chinese call *yang*, and another fluid that is female or lunar known as *Ida*, which in China is

Yin and Yang

known as *yin*. Based on this notion, health is nothing but the result of the right balance of those two fluids or energies within one's organism. And how do we attain such balance? The answer seems to be only one: by learning to breathe in the right manner, something that, according to the yogis, Westerners do very poorly.

According to the yogi doctrine, there are two nervous systems, only one of which operates on the astral plane. This etheric nervous system runs along the spine, establishing close communication with the seven chakras also located along the spinal cord, through which some day, sooner or later, the kundalini energy or snake-like fire—that divine force which, upon reaching the pineal gland to endow the thousand-petal lotus flower with splendor—will mark the exact moment of our spiritual actualization.

Even though Western science does not have answers for the many questions still remaining about the generation, transmission, and nature of the nerve impulse, yogi doctrine does not hesitate to assert that nervous energy is precisely the way in which our body expresses universal energy—that is, prana. Yogi doctrine goes on to say that as the prana or vital force enters our body through both nostrils, it reaches a location behind the midline between the eyebrows, perhaps between the sella turca and the pituitary gland, where it becomes polarized into two elements: ida and pingala, each going to a certain part of the body to tone it up.

When this energy force continues to descend to the coccygeal region, exactly at the base of the spine, it becomes a center of power that is given the name "kundalini," a bipolar manifestation of prana that takes up the form of a caduceus, the staff (the spine) surrounded by two snakes, which currently is the symbol of medicine.

Possibly in the course of years, and perhaps during several lifetimes, the kundalini energy is stored in the perineum, exactly between the anus and the genitalia, in order to later go upward through the whole system of chakras and all levels of consciousness until turning up, like a dazzling flash of indescribable beauty, at the head's highest point.

It turns out to be rather interesting, though still incomprehensible, to know that we are designed to first embark on a descending journey to the human condition, and then another journey in the opposite direction to reach the divinity, or what amounts to the same thing: that we are destined to abandon infinity only to return to it, filled with all the experiences provided by the successive reincarnations. Since the kundalini is stored in the muladhara chakra, that is, the root chakra, near the reproductive organs, it represents the force that lights the flame of sexual desire, not only to perpetuate the species but also to establish an intimate communication with others, to receive the pleasure provided by the opposite sex.

Kundalini is the biblical tree of good and evil: when the energy descends, it may even be forced to satisfy the basest physical appetites, but when it ascends it can give birth to a genius or to a wise man, to the man who has reached the summit of evolution. Kundalini is the enlightenment Buddha talked about, it is a certain promise that man, some day that may even be close at hand, will attain divinity. Hence it is no longer a secret to anyone that the halo surrounding the head of saints is the kundalini "flash."

There are many practices (the use of drugs, among others) to supposedly foster the ascent of the kundalini energy by forcing our way through stages in the evolutionary process, but they all turn out to be dangerous to man's mental stability. The only practice that enables us to awaken that energy force gradually, without running any risk whatsoever, is meditation.

Eyes Half-Closed

Even though many people are accustomed to meditating with their eyes closed, both Buddhists and Taoists have taught that during meditation it is necessary to have one's eyes half-closed and aim one's sight to the tip of the nose in order to fix one's thoughts (or rather the absence of thought) on the point midpoint between the eyes, which Taoists call "the yellow center" and which Buddhists call "the center in the midst of conditions."

This interesting coincidence should be emphasized since in the human face (just like the Sun dominates the forehead, Jupiter the right eye and Saturn the left) the Moon reigns in the middle of both eyes, just where the nose begins, and it is already known that, from the point of view of high magic, as taught by Eliphas Levi, the works of divination and mysteries are under the spell of the Moon.

Indeed, leaving aside the practical aspect of its healthy effects, the act of meditation is ruled by mystery. It has been said that when we pray, God hears our prayers and requests, but that instead, when we meditate, it is we who are able to listen to God's voice. For Edgar Cayce, meditation's greatest achievement did not only lie in propitiating the development of psychic awareness or the acquisition of paranormal powers, but in reaching in that instant the complete abandonment of the physical body, as has happened to those who have had near-death experiences. The true purpose of meditation, therefore, consists of surrendering to a higher power, so that the consciousness of God can inhabit the body of the meditator. In other words: in achieving that one is not the meditator, but that instead Someone (that is, God, the Supreme Being, the Absolute, whatever you want to call Him) is mysteriously meditating us.

Hands on Your Lap

Many yoga treatises say nothing about the position our hands ought to assume while we pray, so usually they are allowed to rest on our lap, at times interweaving our fingers if so desired, or others stretching our arms until our hands touch our knees with our fingers bent. Another way would be by having the thumb and the middle finger touch each other in each hand. Some texts teach that the hands must be placed comfortably on our lap, as we have seen in many statues, that is, with the palm of the right hand over the palm of the left hand, and perhaps with the two thumbs making contact.

In each palm there is an energy-receiving center. Meditating with our palms turned up signifies the desire to ask for protection and assistance to journey inside ourselves. It may also signify asking for help to solve some specific problem, something we need and must obtain.

Even if the meditator does not express any wish (but it is better to express it), streams of universal energy will enter his or her body through the palms, and thanks to this energy wishes will be fulfilled. The Supreme Intelligence comes immediately to provide the meditator with energy, as soon as he or she stretches out their hand to request it.

Tongue Against Your Palate

It has been said that, since very ancient times, Taoist masters became aware that there were two channels conducting energy to all parts of the body. One of those channels, the yin, starts at the base of the spine and goes up through the front part of the body to the tip of the tongue. The other, the yang, goes up through the rear portion, making its trajectory from the perineum to the palate. That is why the tongue is considered like a bridge that can be hanged to connect the two energy streams. When you manage to point your tongue toward the palate and touch it, the two energies become intertwined and flow harmoniously, giving rise to well-being and health.

Of course it is not easy for the meditator, especially at the beginning, to keep the tip of the tongue turned toward the palate. Therefore one should start to meditate while trying to at least keep it close to the teeth. Even though it is best to assume the postures described as faithfully to the ideal as possible, they are not an end in themselves.

We can keep our back straight, our eyes half-closed, place our tongue very close to our palate and control our breathing rhythm, slowing down the rhythm, which does not mean that we have managed to cease our contact with the outer world, to "shut our windows" to the requests by the senses in order to destroy the process of exteriorization, i.e., our communication and exchange with the external world. But don't despair. Pranayana, the control of respiration, enables the meditator to shut her- or himself off to the external world, closing up the flow of sensory information.

Once that first step is achieved, it is not difficult to reach the state called *dharana* by Patanjali, which provides the indispensable concentration to focus our meditating will in a single direction. This concentration is not intended, as many believe, to prevent mental activity but only sensory activity. On the contrary, when attention is focused on a single point, the brain, as Jean Varenne said, "receives a greater amount of intellectual light" (*El Yoga y la tradición hindú*, Plaza & Janes, 1975), opens up in unexpected delight to the subtlest of sensations, and makes the process of enlightenment and the entrance into the kingdom of freedom noticeably easier.

Reasons to Meditate

According to Buddhism individuals may have four reasons to devote themselves to meditative practice:

1. Because their karma predisposes them to meditate.

2. Because they wish to improve their health.

3. Because they deem it indispensable to prepare for a new life and need to grow spiritually.

4. Because they wish to follow the path of Buddha and reach enlightenment.

Usually, meditation is considered an expression of the Eastern religious traditions, whose purpose, as has been said before, is to achieve spiritual enlightenment, just as the Buddha did through the practice of Vipassana meditation. Even though this is true, meditation is also a practice open to all people, and no strict norms have been imposed for anyone to follow. They are only asked to practice it with as much discipline as possible.

We also don't need a rigorous ritual to enjoy the meditative state. Sometimes this state of exceptional pleasantness is reached at the least-expected moment, as we walk through the fields under the canopy formed by the branches of large trees or as we stroll down the beach during a beautiful sunset. We only need, at that unique moment, to be in tune with the sources of universal energy to feel taken over by that supreme tranquility of the spirit, thanks to which at that moment we are purer, more generous, and happier than at any other time in our lives.

Meditation is an activity we perform to achieve a certain objective: to strengthen our immune system, to enhance our creative abilities or to achieve success in some specific areas related to our individual goals, both in the field of professional endeavors and of personal relations with our family and friends.

We meditate because of a spiritual need, to be close to God, but also for many other reasons. Let's consider some of them: '

- Develop inner peace.

- Lessen the devastating effects of stress.

- Learn our previous reincarnations.

- Acquire healing powers.

- Perform astral projections.

- Develop clairvoyance.

- Be successful in love.

- Tap our subconscious.

- Communicate with deceased loved ones.

- Tap fields of more subtle energies, as well as other dimensions we were not aware of.

The Meditator's "Ten Commandments"

1. Once you have made the decision to start meditating, the first thing you must do is select a room where this practice may be performed in as quiet an environment as possible. The room selected for meditation must become a sacred place, in which images of a teacher or a divinity may and should be placed, as well as candles and flowers.

2. When meditating, wear clean, light clothes that are not too tight fitting around your body. It would be preferable to leave your shoes outside the room. Taking off one's shoes and leaving them outside emphasizes the idea that the room intended for meditative practice is hallowed ground.

3. Sit comfortably, preferably on a round cushion, so that your buttocks are raised and your knees can be supported by the floor. Your hands must be together on your lap, with palms turned upward.

4. Keep your back straight, thus taking on a dignified posture and facilitating your breathing rhythm.

5. Place the tip of your tongue against your palate or as close as possible to your teeth.

6. Half-close your eyes, with your sight fixed on an object.

7. Breathe deep and slow. Then breathe normally.

8. Start to pronounce mentally a fitting word for the goal or reason for your meditation, such as Peace, Love, Health, or Compassion.

   You can also use the Tibetan mantra OM MANI PADME HUM. Or simply the primordial sound: OM.

9. Try to keep away bothersome thoughts and daily concerns and fix your attention on a single point: achieve mental concentration. The easiest way to achieve it is to count your breaths successively, both in and out. When you inhale say "one." When you exhale say "two," and so on until counting to ten. Next inhale again and say "one" until counting again until ten, repeating this process as long as you need.

10. Let loose. Let yourself be carried away to the depths of your being. Initiate with happiness this fascinating trip into yourself. At the end of the practice, you must rise slowly and walk silently around the room for five minutes.

Karma and Health

Going back in time, we find that the first individuals who decided to heal others were led to do so by a spiritual vocation. The first shaman or medium that used his or her hands to heal another human being did so while praying. In the Middle Ages monks were devoted to medical research, joining as one both science and religion. In China and Japan spiritual therapy has been practiced while burning incense and pronouncing a mantra.

That may be the reason why at present so many people are dissatisfied with a kind of medical treatment that approaches the patient as an object, and, pressed by a subliminal memory of times past, they long for those magical components and search for alternative healing methods that are the same or similar to the methods used in the dawn of civilization, which involved healing by appealing to faith, to the intercession by a divinity or by invoking the infinite powers of the mind.

In the West the factors triggering numerous diseases are resentment, fear, anxiety, and many other negative emotions. We have medications that can help to ease the burden of these destructive feelings, but no drug can give a definitive solution to the conflicts that cause them and give us inner peace.

Lao-tzu said that a person's well-being depended on that individual's "capacity to return to nature." The practice of meditation makes this possible for us. While meditating all the mental worries caused by our busy modern lives disappear.

By meditating our mind becomes quieter and more alert, free of any ego demands. The ego is the identification with the physical body, with the name we were given when we were born, with the profession we chose, with the pleasures we're after, with the ambitions that arouse us to engage in our daily struggle.

The ego, therefore, has nothing to do with our inner being, which may be referred to by any name (such as the soul, spirit, or subconscious) but is the only thing in us that endures, and it is in this inner being where the wisdom resides that guarantees happiness, health, and self-realization. In India this inner being is called

Shiva, and is said to be sitting in the *Kailas* of the heart. Shiva is the inner teacher whose voice we need to learn to listen to while we dedicate ourselves to the practice of meditation. For Hindus, as already mentioned before, meditation is the most direct way to be able to listen to Shiva's voice.

Meditation is an effective therapeutic technique, since harmony is the same as health, but it is also an ideal method to get to know who we are, where we come from and where we are going.

The Catholic priest François Brune studied the psychic phenomenon of people who managed to survive the actual moment of death. He researched more than one hundred cases of survival in hospital operating rooms, and all of these people later explained that, during the brief period in which they were about to die, they remembered even the slightest details of their lives as in a movie, and that they were also able to travel to places where they lived in their childhood. Harold Sherman, founder of an institution devoted to the research of near-death experiences, also successfully compiled extremely valuable information that made it possible to define the limit between life and death with almost scientific accuracy. Even though these investigations appear to have taken place recently, actually they have always captured the impassioned interest of human beings.

Among the scientific personalities that have been greatly interested in this type of research we must also mention English physicist Sir William Barret, founder of the Society for Psychical Research of London; Elizabeth Kübler-Ross; Raymond Moody, author of the famous book *Life After Life* (Bantam, 1975); Karlis Osis; and Kenneth Ring, a professor at the University of Connecticut who with the co-operation of doctors and nurses at various hospitals successfully gathered numerous testimonies of people who were near death, which were the basis for his book *Life at Death* (Quill, 1982).

They all reported that the persons who came back to life, regardless of whether they were believers or atheists, recounted similar experiences: they enjoyed a state of peace and happiness felt in their earthly lives. Most of them told of having gone through a tunnel at the end of which, within a beam of light, they were greeted by relatives and friends who had passed away long before, who welcomed them with great joy and affection. Many of them also said that the experience had caused an inner transformation whereby they not only lost their fear of death but also, as of that moment, felt the need to intensely seize the time they had left to live, devoting themselves to promoting the happiness of others as a means to achieving their own spiritual development. These phenomena, which have taken place over and over again and not infrequently, have stirred the curiosity of many who are now interested not only in finding out whether the soul is really immortal, but who they were in previous lives.

In the past few years an opinion has become established that many mental disorders of unknown etiology may derive from conflicts not resolved in previous lives. That may be the reason past-life regression therapies have become so relevant. In 1956, Morey Bernstein published *The Search for Bridey Murphy* (Doubleday, 1990), which related the experiences of Virginia Tighe, one of his patients, who during a hypnotic trance asserted that in a previous life her name was Bridey Murphy and she had lived in Ireland. Years later Bernstein traveled to Ireland and was able to verify, after reviewing records and documents, that all the information mentioned by Bridey Murphy with respect to her birth, postal address, and marriage was completely true. More recently the psychiatrist Brian Weis, in his book *Many Lives, Many Masters* (Simon & Schuster, 1988), described past-life regression experiences similar to those reported by Bernstein.

In India, as in most of the East, the opinion has prevailed that the human being consists of a body, which deteriorates and disappears with the passage of time, responding to the Law of Enthropy, and of a soul that is destined to inhabit different bodies in successive reincarnations. Buddhism accepts reincarnation and Buddhist doctrine teaches that an immortal principle named *namshes* gives life to the body. But namshes is not allowed to freely choose the new body that it is to dwell in. That choice is determined by an inescapable law of cause and effect: karma.

According to Buddhism, when someone dies that person goes into a transient state called *Chikhai Bardo*, in which disembodied persons remain for three or four days, not realizing their true condition. They learn they are dead upon entering the second stage called *Chonyid Bardo*, from which they go on to the third stage, *Sidpa Bardo*, where they remain until they initiate a new reincarnation.

A powerful motivation that leads many people to meditation is to acquire knowledge about who they were in previous lives, not only out of innate human curiosity but also because in the study of those lives they may find explanations to many of the conflicts they encounter in their current existence, and by becoming aware of them they may be able to improve their behavior by focusing on not committing the same mistakes they made before, thus relieving any negative aspect of their individual karma.

Inevitably, he who kills by the sword will die by the sword in the next life, in the same way that whoever seduces his friend's wife will pay with exile in his current or future life. You'll always gather as you sow. The past is the future. By knowing who we were, we can get to know what we will be. Of course thanks to effort made and devotion shown it is possible to achieve spiritual enlightenment in a single lifetime, as preached by Buddha, as well as by practicing love, compassion, and altruism. By wishing for our neighbor what we wish for ourselves we can purify our karma, which in practical terms means that we will be spared many of the troubles and sorrow that were in store for us.

How can we access the knowledge about our past lives through meditation? Let's look at one possibility: by using the same resources as the hypnotist uses in past-life regression therapy—that is, by repeating phrases such as this one: "I'm going to travel back in time, beyond time and space, beyond my present life. Who am I now? What's my name? What country am I living in now?"

By knowing our previous lives we can also improve our bodily health. Many organic conditions are caused by some of our actions in a previous reincarnation. If we blinded someone in a previous life, we may now suffer some eye disease. That is only one example of the many conditions that may be caused by our spiritual past. By fixing yesterday's mistakes today we are no doubt improving our current health.

Astral Projections

Others meditate in order to enhance the natural human faculty of performing astral projections, a phenomenon also known as unfolding, extrasomatic experience, bilocation, and out-of-body experience (OBE).

Hindu and Tibetan mystics often talk about these experiences, and Catholic literature contains abundant references to the numerous saints who were seen in two places at the same time. It is known that Saint Anthony of Padua celebrated mass in two convents on the same day at the same time, while Saint Francis Xavier was seen simultaneously on two sea vessels. Other notable bilocations were those of Teresa Neumann and Padre Pio, who performed miraculous cures at a distance by astral projection to the location where the person whom he wished to heal was at the time.

Out-of-body projections often take place without the person intending to, in a spontaneous and unexpected manner. In many cases the departure from the physical body to a distant place takes place even in persons who have no religious training or spiritual interests. While asleep, just as in a dream, they feel taken out of their homes or even out of their city as if a force unknown to them urged them to perform an indispensable task, for the benefit of a person who did not have to actually be a relative or a friend. Often, in the course of these astral projections, they take by the hand a child who is in danger and help him or her find their way home, or prevent a driver from going at full speed ahead, not realizing he or she will encounter a road hazard that will put him or her in harm's way. I have a friend, a person entirely worthy of belief, who told me that during an involuntary astral projection he was able to put out a fire that had started in the kitchen of a nephew. A week later he confirmed that on the same day he had that out-of-body experience a fire was ignited in the kitchen of his nephew's home which miraculously did not spread elsewhere in the house.

Out-of-body projections take place because of the existence of the astral body, which is an exact replica of the physical body that stores our desires and emotions. During the projection the astral body does not separate entirely from the physical one but rather continues to be joined to it by the "silver thread," which will only be cut off should death occur. Although part of the astral body continues to be joined to the physical body in order to participate in the essential functions of the organism, the other part of the astral body enjoys absolute freedom to engage in the most fascinating adventures, able to visit unknown countries and make contact with people of different origins and cultures.

Learning to perform astral projections is not as difficult as you may believe. It could be said it is somewhat similar to learning any new activity. But before you start meditating with this goal in mind, be aware that this training has special requirements. One of them is the diet. Eating and drinking are normal physiological requirements, but for purposes of astral projection it is advisable to at least decrease the amount of food we consume on a daily basis, though not to stop eating for forty days as Moses did on the mountain, or Jesus did in the desert. Anyone who wishes to experience an astral projection must be willing to eat less than usual. A vegetarian diet might be the solution.

The training should preferably take place in the same room used for meditation. You should set out to conduct your practices at the same time, at dusk or in the evening before going to bed. In a perfect state of relaxation, with your eyes closed, start to breathe rhythmically, focusing all your attention on the exhalations, trying to make them as long as possible.

Now you should perform the following visualization: from your solar plexus area a stream of positive energy bursts out, which may be imagined as a powerful beam of light inside which your purest feelings of love, compassion, and altruism travel. Keep those feelings traveling inside the beam of light to the most distant places. Do not make the least effort in trying to imagine those places. Let yourself be led by the light. Allow the light to illuminate freely and spontaneously those places that may be a jungle, a mountainous region, a beach, or a city lighting up at sunset.

This initial practice may be continued for days or weeks, during which you may get the disheartening idea that you are not making any progress in your training. However, inside of you a friendly voice starts to tell you at the time that your goals may be met soon. When you feel ready to take the next step, visualize that you *come out* of yourself through the solar plexus, without the need to confirm whether your astral body remains joined to your physical one through the silver thread. On the contrary, visualize your astral body traveling freely, without encountering a single obstacle in its course, without anything that might prevent its motion. Let yourself be carried out by spontaneity. Allow your astral body to do whatever it pleases (healing a bedridden person or preventing a car accident, for instance) without interference from your will. Rest assured that later on, when you have finished your training, your astral body will obey all of your orders and perform the tasks you assign to it.

When a person experiences an astral projection for the first time, he or she usually fears not being able to return to the physical body, but soon thereafter perceive that he or she is going into a state of ineffable happiness and well-being. This is a report by a man after his first out-of-body experience:

"One afternoon I saw myself suspended in the air, as if the force of gravity did not exist, and I thought that perhaps I was dreaming. However, I looked down and saw my own body sitting on a sofa, with my eyes half-closed but unquestionably awake. Looking at myself, I realized I was experiencing astral travel, just as I had heard. Initially what worried me the most was not being able to return to my physical body at the moment I would try to. I was afraid, but immediately I said to myself that it was not indispensable to go back so soon, that I should wait until I could confirm, as I had heard, that in this state it was possible to move from one place to the other with complete freedom. I felt like walking and indeed was able to as if the air supported me, as I would down any street. All of a sudden, without intending to, I went through the walls of my house and came outside. It was getting dark and the people returning to their homes were passing by me unaware of my presence. Then, over-whelmed by a great feeling of happiness, like a child would experi-ence, I wished I could fly over the rooftops, and immediately saw myself carrying out my wish. How much I have wished for it, be-cause on no other occasion in my life have I been as happy as I was in those moments."

Here is the account of a person who in the course of his medita-tive practice experienced out-of-body projections voluntarily:

"When I learned that it was possible to perform astral projections I was fascinated by the discovery. On an almost daily basis I would try to go into that state of absolute freedom that, furthermore, has noticeably contributed to improve my bodily health. Projecting your astral body is an inexhaustible source of satisfaction because we are able to help other people who are in a difficult situation. On one occasion I found out that a childhood friend, who lived in another city, was in the throes of a deep depression caused by the recent death of his wife. I set out to perform an astral projection to his home in order to help him. I saw myself leaving my physical body as in many other occasions and fly through the air without a set course until I descended into a house that was exactly like my friend's. I saw him sitting on the edge of the bed stroking a hand-gun. I realized he was planning to commit suicide. 'What could I do, my God?' I wondered while I drew near him and started to whisper consoling words. I told him to think of his wife, who in all certainty would not approve of that behavior. It was to be expected that she, from where she was, would rather have him accept her death with resignation and experience the same happiness she wanted to give him during all the time she lived by his side. Well, before a month [went by] I was able to verify that it had not been my imagination. My friend, influenced by his depression, had at-tempted suicide but at a certain moment he thought he heard his wife's voice advising him not to do so."

These out-of-body projections, experienced voluntarily or spon-taneously, reveal to our awareness that it is allowed to act outside the physical body with complete freedom and full control of its fac-ulties, which leads us to think that perhaps it could continue to do so after death takes place.

Directed Meditations

We supposedly acquired the first images dwelling in our mind in our childhood. We are not aware of many of them and at times of almost all of them at the conscious level because they are covered by what Freud called "childhood amnesia," that is, because we have repressed them, just as if we had kept them in a drawer that is now difficult to open. But even if we have repressed them, or perhaps for that very reason, those images do not stop giving constant signs of life, often expressing themselves in dreams through symbols or interfering in our waking consciousness with patterns of behavior that we did not choose yet which determine our relations with others, and, most of the time, as Sri Aurobindo said, causing our illnesses, especially chronic diseases or those that take place repeatedly with a certain frequency.

The philosopher and psychologist Carl Jung went further and said that together with our individual unconscious, which is the reservoir of these images, there is another transpersonal reservoir that he called the "collective unconscious," which provides us with a large number of images belonging to the childhood of the species expressed in ancestral symbols issuing even from other cultures, which nurture us even though they have no relation to us at all. To emphasize this point of view he added: "Just as the human body shows a common anatomy above and beyond any racial difference, the psyche also possesses a common substratum that transcends all differences of culture and consciousness."

What we could call a third group of images dwelling inside of us result from the experiences we've been acquiring throughout our lives and the knowledge we have stored with respect to ourselves and the world around us. All of these images make up our personality and help us decide among the multiple choices we face every day. That is, these images programmed our behavior and, therefore, we have to learn to struggle with them if we really want to learn to know ourselves, achieve full self-control, preserve our psychic and bodily health, and assure a successful performance in our professional life. I have used the verb "to struggle" on purpose because what we are talking about here is indeed developing the ability not only to tune into the images that guide us, but also to engage in a process of active creation of new images that will help us improve our current existence as well as, even though it might seem more difficult, shape our future according to our desires.

Although the past cannot be changed, i.e., the past that is a record of history or events, at least we do know that we can transform our inner past, the past that lives inside of us in the form of images. Many psychotherapists who practice a psychoanalytically inspired method of bringing up the elements of unconscious psychic life to awareness advise the performance of an exercise called "the inner child," which is more or less performed as follows.

In a state of total relaxation, we imagine that we are strolling through a forest, a garden, or some other place in nature where at last we find the child that we used to be. Most likely the encounter will take place during a time in which this child was anxious or afraid, or was subjected to some mental or physical abuse, and by expressing our love, consolation, and support we can remake, if not the painful events, at least the images left by the traumatic situation. The surprising thing is that by expressing love to the child, by strengthening the child's self-esteem, the conflicts may be made to disappear which still burdened the adult because the child had suffered them.

Something similar happens with the so-called "chair technique" used in Gestalt therapy, in which you can imagine sitting on a chair facing another imaginary person—for example, your father. When you have finished talking with your father, you change seats and, assuming your father's role, you answer yourself. This way, by talking in the present about events that took place in the past, conflicts are eliminated, perhaps forever, that may have existed between father and son.

Even though perhaps everybody accepts that most, if not all, of our decisions derive from unconscious images, the controversy is still alive about the exact place where these images are stored. For some this place is located in the brain, specifically the right hemisphere, which is intended not to reason and act methodically like the left hemisphere, but to take us on the wings of imagination and lead us to artistic creativity or to enjoy spiritual values. Instead, for Sri Aurobindo these images are stored in a submerged part of our being where there is no awareness or coherent thought. More recently it has been said that such images are not within us, as everybody thought, but rather kept in the fields of memories and thoughts surrounding us, and that the functions of the brain include specifically tuning in at a given moment to the images in which the brain is interested.

If we want to know how these images shape and decide our behavior, we should start by having a dialog with our subconscious so that what Jung called "the psyche's transcendental function" may take place, that is, narrowing the distance between the rational and the irrational in quest of internal harmony through the unification of opposites. This dialog is likely to lead to success since, if we ask the unconscious for a certain image related to any aspect of our life, the unconscious will honor our request forthwith. The next step would consist of interpreting the image or images given by the unconscious. Dina Glouberman, in her book *Life Choices, Life Changes: The Art of Developing Personal Vision Through Imagework* (Routledge, 1990), offers some examples of how to interpret images stored in the subconscious to use them to our own benefit.

Many meditators confirm that, after a few months of practicing meditation, they learned how to interpret the messages issued by the subconscious, which allowed them to start working with those images to give meaning to and improve their lives. Many of them explained that, when they needed to regain their energy after a long day's work, they tried to imagine they were in contact with nature, lying on the beach, or on soft grass, or swimming in the sea, and that a short time later they would be taken over by a state of relaxation as if they had awakened from a long restful sleep. They also use images to improve their relations with their bosses, imagining they are entering the body of that person to find out what they are thinking about a certain subject or to persuade them to have a more harmonious relationship. They often not only enter the body of people with whom they are friends or have work-related relationships with, but also the body of people already deceased or even of fictional characters who may impart to them wisdom or sagacity. Thus, if they need some guidance, they won't hesitate to enter the body of Albert Einstein or Sherlock Holmes with the certainty that they'll receive the best advice.

Answer yes or no to these three questions:

1. Do you consider yourself able to see yourself with your eyes closed?

2. Do you reach a state of relaxation easily?

3. Do you trust the power of the mind to recover health or achieve success in your endeavors?

Any meditator will answer these three questions in the affirmative. If you gave the same replies, it will be very easy to place those images at your service in all your affairs.

How to Shape Your Future

Many people wonder if there is really a way to harness the energy of our internal universe to reach certain goals. Of course there is. The International Association for Psychotronic Research has devoted itself to teaching methods that may be used to free the infinite power of the energy inside each of us and, by following rules that are not very difficult, to benefit from establishing a direct communication with what Dr. Robert B. Stone calls in many of his books the "Cosmic Psychotronic Generator," which is nothing but universal energy.

Coinciding on many aspects with the Silva Method of Mind Control, Psychotronics recommends imagining a screen like that of a movie theater on which one must visualize the event one wants to come true. Once this practice is completed, one visualizes the happy result of one's wish and enjoys it in advance.

Whether making use of the screen or not, a meditation intended to shape the future entails the following steps:

Sit down comfortably. Relax.

Visualize the event you wish come true.

Visualize all details.

Think of it as intensely as possible, confident that you are the absolute master of your destiny and therefore the result of your visualization will be totally satisfactory.

Think that that future is already waiting for you, such as you designed it.

How to Fight Fear

"When will and imagination are in conflict, imagination will always win out," said Emile Coué, the French hypnotist whose name you will find in any study on how to harness the powers of the mind. From this sentence it follows that if you consume your psychic energy persistently thinking of a harmful habit you want to get rid of, exactly the opposite may happen—your mental attitude will strengthen the habit. The same thing will happen if you extend your index finger and imagine you cannot flex it—no matter how hard you try it will be impossible for you to bend it. By following the law proclaimed by Coué, we can say that whatever manages to become firmly rooted in imagination will always come true on the physical plane, whether it be a feeling of fear or inferiority, or the fervent wish to achieve health or well-being.

There are many feelings that conspire to prevent us from reaching the indispensable mind control we need to perform successfully in life, understanding success not only as the harmonious and gratifying development of the external environment (our financial situation and the image we project to society) but also the radiance expressed in our internal one. Among the feelings that cast the darkest shadow on both environments, the most harmful is fear, which has the most destructive emotional charge. Fear of change, of loneliness, of losing a loved one, fear in any of its manifestations, may be, and no doubt is, the source of almost all diseases and all failures.

The difficulty consists, going back to Coué, because it is impossible to fight fear. Fear is a seven-headed Hydra—so it is useless to cut off any of its heads because they will soon grow back. Fear is a giant whose head no one can cut off because the more we fight it, the stronger it becomes. So how to defeat it, then? By not offering it resistance, by only becoming aware of our true personal worth, by visualizing ourselves, in meditative practice, as persons who react to conflicts fully confident of the victorious results of our efforts by visualizing ourselves as winners in all those activities that awaken our interest. Napoleon never doubted that he was an excellent military strategist. Nor did Mozart ever think he was not a brilliant composer. Neither Goethe nor Dostoevsky nor Flaubert nor Faulkner ever feared that a book they were writing would not be warmly accepted by their readers, and precisely because of that they reached the heights of creativity.

The ability to conquer fear, cast doubts out of our mind, and achieve success lies within us, waiting for the magical moment when our imagination starts the mechanism that causes the unmanifested to manifest itself and intention to turn into action. And one can reach without much difficulty that magic moment when imagination vanquishes fear through the practice of meditation.

Sit down comfortably.

Breathe deeply and slowly. Then return to natural respiration.

Think of a person living or deceased, or some fictional character, who is very important to you for some reason.

Visualize that you "enter" that person's body and assume that person's characteristics: his or her invincible personality.

Part III

Buddhist Meditation

Man's own nature shows the urgency to become
an ever more self-actualized being.

—Abraham Maslow

Within each of us lies
the infinite potential of truth.

—Liliam Rosa Morad

Siddhartha Gautama, who would be known later as Buddha, was born in Lumbini, a small town in the State of Sakyas, son of the Prince Suddhodana and Princess Mayadevi, who died soon thereafter, leaving the child under the care of her sister Mahapajapati, Suddhodana's second wife. History tells us that Siddhartha's father, following tradition, had the priests examine his son and foretell his future.

They soon had an answer: the child had the thirty-two signs of a great man. So he had two possibilities: if he stayed in the palace he would be a just king, but if he left it, attracted to the wandering lifestyle of monks, he would then be a Buddha, who through enlightenment would succeed in escaping the painful cycle of reincarnation.

To prevent the prophesy from becoming true and so that his son would not get to know the dark side of life in all its stark reality, Suddhodana ordered that Siddhartha not be allowed to leave the confines of the palace. Trying to find a way to win over Siddhartha's willing acceptance of his confinement, Suddhodana placed forty thousand female dancers at his service and provided him with eighty-four thousand women. All for naught, because neither dancers nor musicians nor the most beautiful women were able to steer him away from the growing curiosity he felt about the outside world.

Driven by this curiosity, he oftentimes attempted to go to the nearest city, about which he had heard so much, but when he found out that his father had placed guards on all the roads to prevent his escape, he realized that he would only be successful in achieving his purpose if he gained his Suddhodana's consent. Since permission was invariably denied, Siddhartha made use of his great moral reserves and insisted so many times as occasions he had until he managed to overcome his father's resistance. Even though his father gave him his consent, Suddhodana agreed only after taking every precaution so that Siddhartha, on his way to the city, would not meet people who would leave a painful impression on him. However, it was not possible to prevent him, upon passing by some houses, from watching a sick man and an elderly gentleman about to die. Upon concluding, based on his own reflection, that he was subject to the same biological laws as other human beings, and therefore also condemned to sickness and death, Siddhartha underwent a profound inner transformation that led him to become a mendicant monk later on.

Even though it seems to contain many mythical ingredients, this is the historical account of the first years in the life of Siddhartha Gautama. But legend offers a more poetic version when it tells us that he had no need to leave the confinement imposed by his father to realize the sufferings that awaited any person born into this world. One afternoon, as he traveled aboard a carriage around the park located on the grounds of his own palace, the gods allowed a trembling old man leaning on his cane to appear to Siddhartha, soon thereafter followed by a terribly sick man, possibly a leper, next by a dead body, and finally by a monk.

It was not too difficult for Siddhartha to decipher the message: the destiny of everyone, including his own, unavoidably held the three fates: illness, old age, and death. It was also not difficult for him to see that in order to get to know the causes of suffering and to learn how to eliminate suffering, to be above any distress, the only possible solution was to lead a monk's life.

Without saying good-bye to anyone, not even his wife, who had just borne him a son, Siddhartha left the palace and after a thirty-hour walk arrived at the banks of the Anavama River. There he cut off his hair and accepted that, in his new status as a monk, from that moment on to the day of his death he would only allow himself eight objects: three changes of clothes, one belt, a beggar's bowl, a razor blade, a needle, and a sieve to filter water.

Siddhartha Gautama: the Enlightened One

He spent the following six years ardently seeking his spiritual actualization. He first received the teachings of two yoga masters: Alara Kalama and Rudraka Ramaputra, who Siddhartha thought could show him the way to salvation. But he was soon dissatisfied and left his teachers to try to find his own path. He subjected his body to the harshest mortification, often holding his breath and depriving himself of all nourishment. He abandoned this unyielding austerity he had imposed upon himself when almost at the point of death he realized that such mortification practices were useless. Not wasting any time, he bathed in the river, ate a little rice, and sat beneath a tree, intent on remaining there until he found himself in the deepest reaches of his heart.

At last, one full-moon night in May he fulfilled his aspirations. That night, seated on a kusha grass cushion, in a state of meditation, he ceased to be Siddhartha Gautama and became the Buddha, "the Awakened One," "the Enlightened One." At dawn his innumerable reincarnations in different times and places were still going through his mind, as if projected on a movie screen, and while the Wheel of Life turned so he could glimpse all his successive deaths and rebirths, it was given for him to learn that attachment and desire were the source of all suffering and that only by defeating them could humans escape the painful cycle of life and death. That radiant morning would be a gift for all humanity, since the privilege of being cognizant of the dharma, the teaching, the liberating knowledge, would now and forever be accessible to everyone. If they persevered they would be able, like Buddha, to achieve enlightenment.

The answers that he could not obtain by asking wise men or mortifying his body were discovered by Siddhartha through meditation. From that moment on, for forty-five years to his death, Buddha preached his doctrine, which is expressed in the Four Noble Truths: *Suffering, Its Cause, Its Cessation,* and the *Path that Leads to Its Cessation.* To Buddha suffering means "being born, growing old, falling sick, being joined to what you don't love, being separated from what you love." To him life itself was not painful. It was because man was entangled in the nets of illusion, because man had not liberated himself from the false mirages that tied him to desire. Desire, he taught, leads to action and when this action, as often happens, does not produce the expected results, then it is followed by anguish and therefore by a new desire to act in order to escape the suffering caused by dissatisfaction.

A teaching emerges from Buddha's doctrine: to escape from the bondage of desire, which always leaves you dissatisfied, the only possible option lies in achieving complete spiritual actualization, which, according to his own doctrine, is not attained by divine intercession but through a practice derived from the human condition. Enlightenment, in Buddhism, is a personal experience. "Be unto yourself as it is a lamp. Rely on yourself. Don't depend on anyone else," proclaimed Buddha. This does not mean that a Buddhist's intention should be to achieve a contemplative state that will estrange him from the world, disregarding other people's problems and suffering. Quite the contrary. Buddhism, as stated by His Holiness the Dalai Lama, denies the independent existence of the self. It teaches us to rejoice over the happiness of others. It postulates that we are constantly exchanging information, not only with other people but also with things.

To a Buddhist, the notion of interdependence cannot be overlooked: what affects me affects you and affects the rest of humanity, animals, and plants, as well as objects we consider inanimate. A thought is like a stone thrown into a river: the waves it causes expand to infinity, interwoven with other thoughts that apparently belong only to other people. You are never alone, not even when you meditate in solitude, because at that moment your meditation benefits other people. Your meditation benefits others who have not yet learned to meditate. You are paving the way for them to also reach enlightenment.

Buddhism offers two traditional meditation forms: in the first, called *Samatha meditation*, its aim is concentration, and in the second, called *Vipassana meditation*, its purpose is to develop understanding. Samatha meditation is practiced with a colored disk, which may be red, white, yellow, or blue, located around ten to fifteen feet lower than the meditator's eyes. After looking at the disk intently for several seconds, you close your eyes, focusing your attention on the memory of the disk, which remains on the retina for a while longer until it starts to vanish. This process of opening your eyes, looking at the disk intently and then trying to recover the image, feeling it vibrating inside of us with the evoking force, turns into a fascinating exercise that must be repeated throughout the course of the meditation.

While you continue to half-open your eyes to observe the disk and close them again to remember it, the meditator must focus his attention on his breathing rhythm and repeat a phrase or mantra. The disk, the breathing and the repetitive sound are only an aid to achieving concentration. Having completed this step, already in a true state of ecstasy accompanied by an ineffable happiness, the meditator usually perceives an internal image, which may very well be a statute of Buddha, a picture of Christ, or any of the various divinities of the Tibetan Pantheon. After observing any of these images intently and fervently, you then allow it to vanish slowly.

One of the extraordinary effects of Samatha meditation is that it may lead to ecstasy, a state that for Saddhatissa meant the loss of conceptual thought in favor of pure consciousness. The other aspect of Samatha meditation is related to miracles. For Buddhists these miracles, such as levitation, the gift of healing or the gift of ubiquity, did not take place through divine intervention but as a result of man's spiritual development.

The practice of this meditation generates miraculous powers, but the meditator must abstain from developing these faculties in order to gain fame or admiration. Lao-tzu had already given this warning: "Those who boast about their powers will lose them." One must strive not to show off these faculties, even in order to instill faith in others. Even though he healed the sick and multiplied loaves and fishes, Jesus Christ refused on many occasions to perform miracles, thinking that faith induced by miracles is not true faith, and that his followers must be guided in their path to perfection only by their own experience. Buddha preached something similar.

If Samatha meditation's purpose is to reach a state of concentration, the aim of Vipassana meditation is closely related to the process of enlightenment. It must be initiated, just as Samatha meditation, by focusing on your breathing rhythm, but at an even deeper level that will enable you to discern the actual development of respiration, as for example, the thermic alternation that takes place when we breathe in cold air and breathe out warm air. As meditation proceeds, the difference between Samatha and Vipassana meditation becomes more obvious. If during Samatha meditation the meditator should attempt to stay away from the demands made by the environment, for example, the external noise or smells coming from a nearby garden, in turn in Vipassana Meditation those same noises or smells become the object of meditation. Noise—who or what makes it? The smell—where does it come from? Where is that garden? Is it far away or nearby?

Satori

It is not possible in this book to give a satisfactory explanation of the scope of Vipassana meditation, in which attention does not remain focused unidirectionally on a certain point. In this meditation, the meditating individual then becomes part of his panoramic vision. We recommend that the meditator be assisted by a teacher experienced in the performance of this practice, at the end of which we'll find ourselves at the start of the Path, which in Zen is called *satori*, a road leading to another plane of consciousness where we start to see everything under a new and amazing light.

Psychic Powers

If we used the phrase "a place that is not a place" to refer to a zone of our inner world from which we can exert a decisive influence on our health, you would probably smile incredulously. "If that place does not exist, how is it possible that it could exist?" you would ask yourself, exhausting all the reasonings of Cartesian logic. However, we can find an answer to this question not in mysticism but in modern physics.

Atoms, as we all know, are made up of subatomic particles, but those particles, according to quantum mechanics, paradoxically don't exist truly as objects, but only as "tendencies to exist." A subatomic particle is a "quantum," that is, a certain *amount* of something, but this something has only the consistency of an illusion: it is both mass and energy simultaneously.

The same thing occurs when we meditate, when we start that fascinating voyage to the depths of our true self. We reach a place that no one has been able to find but which holds all our creative abilities, all the wisdom acquired in this lifetime and in previous existences—a place where not only is our individual memory stored but all the memories of the species, joined by a common heritage. Jung expressed this idea when he wrote about patterns of consciousness inherited throughout thousands and thousands of years of human experience, saying that our psyche is inhabited by a Wise Old Man, thousands of years old, who knows and remembers everything.

People who meditate with the aim of expanding their psychic consciousness should start by having a fluid communication with that Old Man that Jung spoke of. Since he symbolizes wisdom, we can ask him all the questions that come to mind, with the certainty that we will always get a satisfactory answer. The first questions could be: is it worthwhile to strive toward awakening our psychic powers? Does a paranormal faculty of knowledge really exist? The answer will surely be in the affirmative—that's the answer given to all those who have asked the Old Man on this subject.

Paranormal powers are natural faculties that a human being possesses, abilities that have been forgotten or that are often used inconsistently, hardly being aware that the Old Man that dwells within us helped us to solve a problem. The ideal thing is for individuals to be able to actualize all their latent capabilities, provided the use of these abilities responds to the highest spiritual aspirations. Arthur Ford said, "To those who long after paranormal powers my advice is unequivocal: either they develop a higher motivation or they ought to quit immediately. The consequences of a deliberate misuse of these abilities can be disastrous."

Edgar Cayce, who was in favor of everyone developing their psychic abilities, emphasized that the use of these powers was only advisable when these people became conscious of what he called "unitary reality"—that is, when they acquire the conviction that they are one with God, when they are able to love God with all their heart.

To all those who aspire to awaken their psychic powers, Cayce advised them that as a first step they must learn to cooperate. Co-operation, to Cayce, meant laying down a bridge of harmony not only to others but also and especially with that "unitary reality" that binds us forever with God. The more we advance toward higher states of consciousness, allowing new aspects of the Infinite Intelligence to operate in us, the higher will be the probability, according to Cayce, of experiencing extrasensory perceptions.

Since meditation is possibly the most adequate way to connect with Infinity, it also turns out to be the most effective method to increase many paranormal psychic powers. Indeed, there is no doubt that meditation awakens and strengthens extrasensory perception. Many Buddhists who practice Samatha have proved it for themselves.

The first thing you gain by meditating is quieting down your mind, an absolute inner peace and an ineffable sense of restfulness. This sense of restfulness cannot escape from the laws of impermanence, however, and therefore it is only a way to prepare yourself for the start of a new path; to be able to change and adapt to the new situations. While we are in the midst of this intoxicating calm, this period of tranquility, we are more able than ever to quicken our underlying capabilities, of which we were hardly aware. By meditating we can suddenly discover that we are what we are, but also what we can be, and already are, a much brighter person than we suspected.

Extrasensory Perceptions

Ever since the first vestige of intelligence arose in the universe, there have been extrasensory perceptions—man's own nature produces them, if we could apply the verb "produce" to something that flows spontaneously without the intervention of our conscious will and requiring not even the least effort. Going back in time to the first humans who populated the Earth, we would watch them painting on the walls in the caves of Lascaux and Altamira. These prehistoric drawings, dating back twenty thousand years before our time, reflect magical rituals inspired by extrasensory perceptions. The Bible, the writings and experiences of Paracelsus, Francis Bacon, Cagliostro, Cristian Rosenkreutz, and Teresa de Ávila represent direct historical occurrences of incidents involving paranormal psychic powers.

The year 1882, when the Society for Psychical Research was founded in London, marked the real start of the history of parapsychology and, therefore, of the systematic study of these phenomena, for which no explanation could be found till then. In a treaty on metaphysics published in Paris in 1923, Charles Richet gave the name of *cryptesthesia* to paranormal knowledge. Van Rijnberk, of Amsterdam University, called them "receptor" phenomena, while Louise Rhine of Duke University preferred the term "extrasensorial perception," which was finally accepted and standardized during the First International Parapsychology Congress, at the University of Utrech in Holland in 1953.

Extrasensory perception, also known as "ESP," is a series of cognitive phenomena whereby a person obtains information without the presence of known physiological receptors. ESP comprises phenomena such as clairvoyance, telepathy, precognition, psychokinesis and cryptomnesia, all of which can be furthered by the practice of meditation, something that was already known from the first experiments carried out by Charles Honorton of Princeton University, and by Gertrude Schmeider of New York City College.

Intuition

A moment comes, without consulting logic or conducting any reasoning, in which from the depths of our awareness an idea quickly surfaces which arrives precisely at the right time to offer a way to solve a certain situation satisfactorily. Where did this idea, this knowledge, come from? How is it possible that some kind of inner voice gave us the solution to a problem without our being aware how this came about? Did Jung's Wise Old Man provide us with the answer?

Without a doubt there is an information package containing infinite wisdom codified in our DNA from the very moment that the sperm fused with the egg to begin our existence. But it is even more extraordinary that each of us, in a fraction of a second, is able to organize this information in order to use it to solve a certain problem.

The problem could have also been solved by reasoning, but, as if someone wanted to spare us the effort, the knowledge needed came in an unexpected way. That's what we know as intuition. We could find many other definitions of it. Perhaps a very expressive definition of intuition is that of Henry Miller when, referring to his literary work, he confessed: "I obey my own instincts and intuition. I know nothing in advance. Often I put down things which I do not understand, secure in the knowledge that later they will become clear and meaningful to me. I have faith in the man who is writing, who is myself, the writer."

Edgar Cayce considered intuition the highest expression of ESP and emphasized that it was preferable to develop intuition over any other form of extrasensory perception. He insisted on this point of view not only because intuition confirms our fluid communication with our inner self, but because at the same time it provides information, it reveals an amazing creative capacity. Indeed, intuition not only contributes an idea but the way to put it in practice, thus inducing us to correct our bearings, discover new aspects of a given situation and start a change that will foster a new constellation of events that will be unquestionably beneficial to us.

We must rely on that creative capacity always. To that end, to strengthen our intuition, we recommend the following meditation.

The Answers of the Wise Old Man

Close your eyes. Relax.

Imagine your heart wrapped in a blue flame.

Focus all your attention on that flame.

Without making the slightest effort, have the flame grow with a light blue color occupying all areas of your body—your chest, belly, and head.

Try to think only of that blue light that has invaded all the organs of your body, filling them with an unbelievable serenity.

That serene feeling is health.

Even though the main goal of this meditation is not necessarily to keep healthy, be aware that we must pay attention to our body's well-being. Your body is a temple. Take good care of it.

Now imagine that far away in the distance, as if it emerged from the blue light, a diminutive figure slowly advancing toward you starts to take shape. The figure keeps growing and growing until it becomes large enough for you to recognize who it is: it's the Wise Old Man that lives inside of you, the symbol of all your inner wisdom.

The Wise Old Man may be a corpulent man, with a long white beard, blue eyes, and pink cheeks, almost like Santa Claus, or a thin Old Man, flexible like a bamboo reed. He may be similar to one of your grandfathers, or remind you of any other elder you may have seen in the park one day.

Start by greeting him and showing him you're glad he's there.

Ask him your first questions, the most simple ones, those requiring only a yes or no answer.

The Wise Old Man will give you these first replies by slightly nodding or shaking his head to indicate whether his answers are affirmative or negative. With time and practice you will get to hear his voice.

You can inquire about any aspect of your life, asking him for guidance and advice.

The Wise Old Man will offer the exact solution to the problem that motivated you to ask him.

Thank him for his answers and allow the Wise Old Man to return, little by little, to the depths of the blue light.

Intuition and the New Age

You don't need to be a master intuitive or a clairvoyant to realize that the grave crises that our planet is currently going through are due to an inevitable process of readjustment before reaching the New Age. But no doubt the psychic powers, and most especially intuition, will be very useful to those who want to contribute to the physical manifestation of the astral designs conceived by the Cosmic Masters to create the conditions that will allow Bodhisattva Maytreya to return to Earth.

It is known that numerous masters have taken up physical bodies in India, Russia, North America, and Central Europe. It is also known that Masters Hilarion and El Morya will reappear in various countries in order to facilitate the Divine Plan foretold for the Age of Aquarius. *Millenarianism* refers to the belief in the coming of a historical period which will set the start, or which has already started, a millennium of peace and happiness on Earth in the new Age of Aquarius, during which God will reveal himself directly to the hearts of all men and women. The belief in a New Age postulates that man will return to his original condition, i.e., that of Adam and Eve, and this will enable him to acquire a new consciousness that, according to Gioacchino da Fiore, will be "the coming true of every human being's dream: a happy, healthy, balanced, pleasant, and abundant life."

This New Age is astrologically identified with the transit of the constellation of Aquarius to occupy the position held by the constellation of Pisces. The Pisces cycle was characterized by an attachment to political ideologies and to fanaticism, while the Aquarius cycle announces a fluid relationship with nature and with our own bodies, as well as the development of human potential abilities, most of which are still unexplored. Among the skills that have already reached noticeable development at the threshold of the New Age we find the use of the power of the mind to heal disease, to solve problems in areas as specific, among others, as love relationships, artistic creativity, and work performance, and also to attain higher states of consciousness that will enable us to experience cosmic love and, of course, achieve spiritual enlightenment, such as the states reached through the practice of meditation.

There are numerous people interested in esoteric studies that eagerly yearn to establish spiritual contact with any of the members of the hierarchy who have designed and are designing the new millennium of happiness and peace. Intuition, strengthened by meditation, will enable them to lay the groundwork for this communication to occur, since it will not take place, of course, unless the candidate shows absolute obedience to the instructions of his teacher.

Perhaps the candidate may find guidance to facilitate this communication if he or she pays close attention to the following message, which may have been offered by a Member of the Hierarchy:

The Twelve New Words

1. My Only Law Is Love.

2. My Only Command Is to Fulfill Your Sacred Mission.

3. My Only Word of Encouragement Is That a Reward Awaits You.

4. My Only Order Is Not to Deny Me.

5. My Only Smile Will Be for Those Who Follow Me.

6. My Only Praise Will Be for Those Who Fulfill Their Mission.

7. My Only Recognition Will Be for Those Who Reach the Light.

8. My Only Child Will Be Whoever Says: "I Am God on Earth."

9. My Executing Hand Will Be Used Only Against the Evil.

10. My Only Purpose in My Thirst for Justice Will Be to Destroy Oppression.

11. My Commanding Voice Will Only Be Used to Lash Out at Those Who Do Harm.

12. My Only Blessing Will Be for You, and You Will Be My Light.

Part IV

The Warrior's Rest

Be loving, start listening to
your inner voice, and follow it.

—Sai Baba

Humankind has lost its internal paradise, which is equivalent to the biblical garden in which God placed Adam and Eve at the beginning of time. This ontological deficiency has been the cause of all their conflicts: they know that they need to recover something because they experience an estrangement alien to their nature, because they have not been able to accept their loss, because they dream constantly of gaining back a landscape where the juiciest fruits hung from the trees at arm's reach. They dream nonstop of returning to their starting point where happiness, inner joy, and full actualization await them, but simultaneously, as they dream of this paradise lost, they fall prey of the deepest disappointment as if they suddenly became aware of their captivity, of the human condition that denies them any possibility to return to the Promised Land.

The answer then given by their vanity, by their wounded pride, is to boast about everything they have apparently achieved throughout history, all the conquests attained by the civilization they have set in motion. That is why modern humankind is constantly trying to justify their behavior, deny that there was any loss, and even declare they are satisfied with their limitations because, thanks to those, they have been able to create an objective world that in a certain way provides them with protection.

To escape the troubles brought on by their nostalgia, humankind has created inviolable categories that lead them into an ever-more dual world: light and shadow, love and hate, war and peace, altruism and selfishness. This duality turns the individual into a hero while it also requires him or her to take sides. Since the battle does not take place around them but inside of them, the fierce struggle that ensues deep within the self eventually tears him or her apart. They are grateful (or think they are) to this duality that denies them inner peace for the sense of possession with which it endows them: what's "mine" versus what's "yours," my piece of land versus my neighbor's, a notion that sometimes justifies and provides them with the adventure of fighting in favor of the aggrieved party, and on not a few occasions with the consolation of thinking that justice has prevailed in their physical environment and that each person is in possession of what that person was able to acquire, thanks to his or her intelligence, willingness, and efforts.

Man deceives himself because, as Castaneda said, "the other worlds are as possessive as our own." Even if he appears to accept the rules of the game imposed by the objective world and dictated by his reason, he knows that at some unforeseen moment he must make the jump, leave behind the realm of duality and acknowledge that life is a fabric in which each thread and each empty space call for interdependence. Indeed, there can't be night without day, life without death, or sound without silence. This is a jump in which both cerebral hemispheres take part at once: the left hemisphere, which before the jump would reason by itself, and the right hemisphere, which enabled him to soar on the wings of imagination. In this jump the personality does not die but is rather transformed: the jump of a nondual person who at last managed to integrate all of his or her parts.

It was not lost on me that this jump could only be made by means of the techniques to which Orientals had devoted themselves for centuries. Nor was I unaware that meditation activated the body's repair system and that many of my meditating friends enjoyed excellent health, irradiated contagious happiness,and were successful in their affairs.

I could not deny that I would benefit from this technique. However, something prevented me from enthusiastically recommending it to others. "If the wrong man uses the right means, the right means will do wrong," says the Chinese proverb. Many years ago, way before I started to write this book, I used to think that these Oriental teachings, in spite of their wisdom, might not find their way successfully into the life of Western people. Could modern human beings, the high executive of a multinational corporation, the businessperson, the advertising agent, the agricultural engineer, our next-door neighbor, that man or woman who goes to a flower shop, drives a car at top speed, is a football fan, and at the end of the day sits down in front of a TV set—can that person, I wonder, reach samadhi the way an Oriental, a yogi, or a lama would, who were taught the art of meditation by their parents and grandparents since their earliest childhood? However, after so many reflections, the answer was in the affirmative. Carl Jung asserted that just like the human body has a common anatomy above and beyond racial differences, so the psyche has a common substratum that transcends all differences of culture and consciousness.

This unconscious psyche, common to all humanity, was also revealed by Max Lüscher in his classical study on analyzing personality traits based on color perception. Lüscher underscored the existence of a sensory language that enables everyone to perceive the same colors the same way, regardless of their cultural background. People of all cultures get excited when they see red while the color blue soothes them. It has been shown that in anyone, regardless of nationality or ethnicity, who watches the color blue for a long time, respiration will become slower and blood pressure will drop.

So then, why doubt that we Westerners can make use of the tools employed by Orientals to achieve internal harmony and maintain health by relaxation and meditation techniques? Happily, that doubt has apparently been left behind. Now it is simply left for us to engage with discipline and happiness in these practices that have always shown their efficacy since humans first postulated that opposites always balance each other out and therefore arrived at the conclusion that the eternal struggle between sleep and wakefulness would give rise to a new state of consciousness achieved through meditation. This practice allows us to recover the energies lost during our exhausting daytime schedule without losing control of our conscious mind, remaining as alert as when we are awake.

Whenever someone accepts a master or guru to teach her or him how to meditate, the teacher will immediately tell that person that she or he must accept the discipline of meditating daily at the same time. It is advisable to meditate three times a day: early in the morning, at noon and in the evening. If anyone finds it impossible to comply with these requirements, then that person must at least make an effort to do his or her meditation in the morning, which is the most fruitful type of meditation and which should ideally be performed between three and four A.M., the time called by Hindus *Brahma Muhurta*, or God's Hour.

In any event, whether you meditate in the morning or at night, the important thing is setting a fixed time for your meditation. "God and you must agree on a specific time for your daily meeting," said Sri Chinmoy to emphasize the importance of discipline in the meditative practice. In order to make this task easier for modern individuals, yogi Maharishi Mahesh stressed that with two fifteen- to twenty-minute daily sessions it is possible to obtain the benefits afforded by meditation. The Maharishi even expressed the opinion that people with very demanding professions could practice meditation anywhere where they were, whether it be a bus, a train, or a waiting room.

The perfect thing would be to do it in a room of our own home where no one could disturb us or distract us, and, especially, to do it while sitting on a cushion, with our knees bent, so the hips would be higher than the knees, which must rest on the floor. If the meditator can't adapt to this posture, then he or she may meditate while sitting comfortably on a chair.

Well, let's begin:

Keep your back as straight as possible.

Half-close your eyes, fixing your sight on a place located slightly above the tip of your nose.

Start to breathe deeply and slowly.

Breathe in. Breathe out.

Try to pause for an ever-longer time after each exhalation.

If you manage to do this, you'll notice that the rhythm of your breathing slows down. Yogis are of the opinion that making these pauses as long as possible prolongs longevity and unquestionably will noticeably improve your health.

Logically, inhaled air cannot reach your body beyond the lungs. But you already know that air is bipolar, that there are two fluids: oxygen and prana, i.e., universal energy. And you can indeed make this energy go and reach wherever you want.

By visualizing this energy, you can succeed in having it traverse your whole body. Guide it to your belly, to your pancreas, down to your intestines.

After being attentive to your breathing rhythm and taking possession of the light, you'll surely feel totally relaxed.

This is the right moment to begin repeatedly focusing on one word, sound, or prayer. Each time you breathe in you must repeat as many times as you can the word chosen, which may be "love" or "health" or "peace," depending on your reason or goal for meditation. You can also repeat the word "one," as advised by Edgar Cayce, in order to increase your feelings of empathy with others, the wish to "be one" with somebody else, to be one with the All.

You can also meditate by listening to the OM, the eternal verb, the primordial sound, which, as taught by the Upanishads, is "similar to the ringing of a bell sounding from afar," and which, according to the actual Vedic texts, may lead to the contemplation of the Absolute. They teach that we need to meditate by concentrating on the OM syllable, in which we recognize the Lord himself.

The dissolution of the mental activity that connects us with the outer world is a task that requires a long period of learning. Even though meditation is a natural human function, a faculty that humankind has refused unexplainably to continue to develop, the most difficult task we really need to succeed in is the cessation of mental activity, so we can focus our attention on only one point, reaching the state that Patanjali called *dharana*, which may be translated as "mental concentration." When you achieve dharana, which means stopping the unremitting barrage of pesky sensory perceptions, our thinking goes on, against what might be expected. "Just as postures do not suppress the life of the body," wrote Jean Varenne, "attention does not imply the dissolution of mental activity." Quite the contrary. During dharana the brain, no longer a slave to the outer world, attains its greatest splendor—you think most subtly and intuitions flow with amazing ease.

Just as the path leading to dharana or to mental concentration is strewn with difficulties, it is not an easy task either to find a mental image that will serve as support for meditation. Buddhists tend to meditate on divinities—for example, any of the five Supreme Healers: Amoghasiddhi, Amitaba, Vairochana, Akshobya, and Ratnasambvava. When Buddhists meditate on a divinity they don't visualize it immediately in all of its details, but rather gradually: first, perhaps, the cushion on which the divinity is sitting; next its feet, the dress it is wearing, until little by little visualizing it fully.

The same process is carried out when meditation is performed on a mandala, which means "circle," the geometrical representation that will most easily lead to the dissolution of "pesky mental activities." In Vajrayana Buddhism the mandala is a graphic representation of the pure sphere which a Buddha inhabits and stresses the notion that the world around us and around our mind are part of the same continuous experience. When meditating on a mandala the same operation is performed: the elements making up the mandala must be remembered gradually until, as if in a jigsaw puzzle, you manage to put together all of its parts.

Mandalas are symmetrical shapes that usually assume the form of a circle, a square, a triangle, et cetera. These symbols, which have found their way into all religious initiations since times immemorial, constitute one more confirmation of the validity of Jung's "collective unconscious" theory: in different communities the same mandalas arose. The simultaneous appearance of similar mandalas in different cultures and communities nowadays takes on a growing archeological and anthropological interest. Common traits, for example, between the Egyptian and Mayan cultures, represent an enigma that will continue to spur our curiosity. The same thing

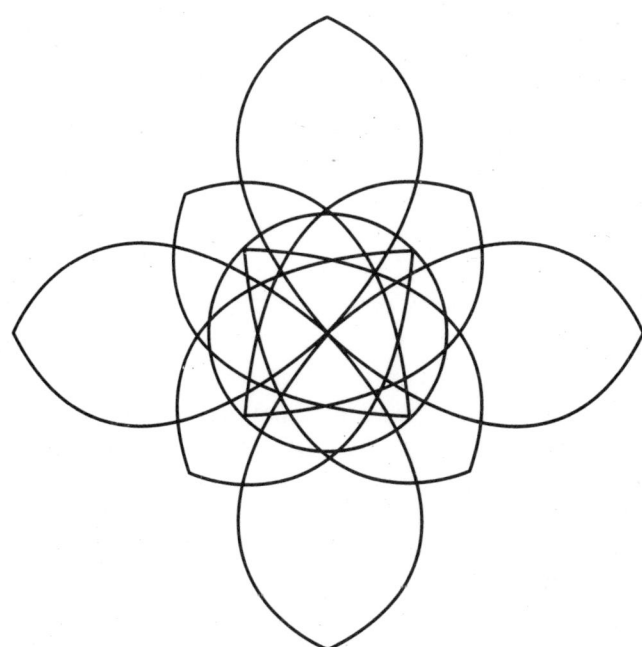

Mandala

happens with cruciform symbols that turn up in cultures as dissimilar as the Tibetan and Mexican cultures.

A moment comes in which the meditator realizes that the ultimate goal of his or her practice is as easily available as opening a door to which you have the key. He or she has succeeded in controlling the rhythm of their breathing, has attained the cessation of "pesky mental activities," has left behind the sensory perceptions that tied him or her to the external world, and has finally reached dharana, the indispensable mental concentration to focus attention on only one point.

Therefore, the only thing left is to descend and descend until reaching the very bottom of the unknown self. Then the meditator, as if losing self-control, experiences a pleasant sensation of searching for roots, for his or her inner paradise, until he or she feels they can let go or transcend, abandoning all contact with their body, and then go beyond their sensory perceptions, well beyond personal desires, feelings of struggle and dread, of the anger and fear that populate waking moments and dreams, penetrating ever deeper into the quiet and the light, into the enclosure where all mental disturbances start to weaken and vanish, plunging ever deeper into a place where hate starts to diminish because love increases, where anger decreases as compassion augments.

When you reach this state of true ecstasy, you enter fields of energy that may not have been perceived by everyday reasoning: it is a place that is not a place, where thought is transformed into pure consciousness, a different world where there can be no fear, concerns, or un-happiness, a zone in which we can exert a decisive influence on cellular intelligence and maintain our good health.

How to Master Stress

It is no exaggeration to assert that any disease can be prevented if we are able to keep our internal harmony and by supporting the quiet, patient, and inalterable work of cellular intelligence. In the deepest reaches of our being we have the almost miraculous capacity to restore health. One of the factors that conspire most harmfully against internal harmony is stress and for that very reason it is also the cause of numerous illnesses.

Today everybody knows what stress is. Busy modern living is constantly causing it and it is frequently commented on. Often we hear a friend or acquaintance complain that he or she is "stressed out." Stress may be caused by any concern, fear, or feeling of anguish. It may turn up when we wish for something and are not able to get it, when there is the threat of a vehicular accident, when a loud noise is suddenly produced close to us, when we think that for some unknown reason we might lose our employment.

Stress threatens us every day, at all times. It is a reality suffered by everyone—some to a greater extent than others. Very few people manage to escape the havoc created by stress in our internal environment. We suffer from stress, but perhaps very few get to know for sure the dangers entailed by it. Very few are sufficiently prepared to overcome this perhaps irreparable peril that awaits us in ambush.

When we are subjected to one or more stress factors, the adrenal glands secrete so-called stress hormones, among them adrenaline and cortisol, which turn our normal anabolic metabolism (energy-generating) into catabolic metabolism, which consumes all the energies and usually induces hypertension, diabetes, and osteoporosis as well as a weakening of our immune system. To fight these and other destructive processes caused by stress, modern science is already accepting the notion that people live in two states of consciousness (wakefulness and sleep) and can only liberate themselves from the stress factor if they are able to achieve a third state: meditation, which not only will enable them to reach a very high degree of muscle relaxation but also attaincontrol over their physiological functions.

In 1950 a new theory closely related to stress started to gain acceptance: the theory of free radicals, that the oxygen atoms that play an important and beneficial role in the immune system were the same ones that caused damage to the human body by uniting with and oxidizing cholesterol. It is true that Nature, always trying to achieve a balance, generates under normal conditions the same amount of free radicals and antioxidant enzymes. When this equilibrium is broken, in most cases it is then too late and practically useless to turn to other antioxidants such as vitamins C and E, and it is almost impossible to counteract the destructive influence of free radicals unless we manage to restore a physiological balance, whereby health will result again from the work of cellular intelligence. The mind can take control of involuntary functions only through such techniques as offered by Hatha yoga, meditation, or the free flowing of energy throughout the organism through the Tao.

The concept of stress, since it was formulated for the first time in 1930, has changed with time. Nowadays we know that not all people react to stress the same way, but we also know that even the most innocuous situations may causes the muscles in our body to tense up and upset our breathing rhythm, obvious signs that stress is turning up in our life. The reactions that take place when facing this stress cause changes in our brain chemistry. These chemical substances, secreted in an uncontrollable manner, may in turn cause cardiovascular disease, depression, and even cancer. Fortunately they don't have to have a necessarily harmful effect on our body. Brain chemistry may also have a positive influence on health if we learn the art of keeping in our mind only positive thoughts. In the same way feelings of sadness or anger weaken the body's resistance to disease, experiencing love, happiness, generosity, and compassion causes profound physiological changes that immediately translate into health and well-being.

It may be useful to ask yourself the following questions:

YES/NO

1. Do you suffer from headaches?   _____

2. Breathing difficulties?   _____

3. Palpitations?   _____

4. Panic attacks?   _____

5. Do your hands shake?   _____

6. Are your muscles tense? _____

7. Do you get too tired? _____

If you answer yes to most of these questions, you should start doing some relaxation exercises and, of course, learn to meditate. These are symptoms of anxiety. They also confirm, furthermore, that you are stressed out.

The art of relaxation at the heart of Hatha yoga is currently being used by Western scientists to cure numerous diseases, among them functional neuroses, asthma, ulcers, colitis, sleep disorders, and hypertension. A method most commonly employed is known as Jacobson's technique or progressive relaxation, which begins by having the patient contract his or her muscles before concentrating on the process of relaxation. This contraction and relaxation technique is very similar to the exercise that follows.

Learning to Relax

The first step toward mastering stress is learning to relax. Relaxation is not the ultimate response to conflicts, but it is a good start. Relaxation is a technique that must be practiced with discipline. It is the opposite of stress and an effective tool to fight it.

If you want to learn to relax, you must accept the same requirements that apply to meditation: select a room where you can do your exercises in the utmost quiet. You must devote fifteen to thirty minutes to this practice on a daily basis. Sit on a chair or lie on your back on a bed.

Breathe deeply and slowly. Then go back to your natural breathing.

Close your eyes or, if you prefer, fix your attention on a distant object.

Commence the exercise with your right leg. Tense your toes and your calf muscles, then suddenly relax them.

Now do the same thing with your left leg.

Focus your attention on your pelvic region. Picture that area of your body becoming relaxed the same way your legs and feet did.

Try to have that warm and pleasant sensation of relaxation go up to your belly. Think that all your belly muscles are loose and relaxed.

Now tense your shoulder muscles and suddenly relax them. Enjoy the pleasant sensation that spreads through this area of your body.

Concentrate on your neck. Tense it. Suddenly relax it.

This pleasant sensation of relaxation experienced in your neck now should move up to your head. Tense the muscles in your face and suddenly relax them.

Before concluding this exercise breathe deeply and slowly. Go back to your normal respiration.

And Now, Start to Meditate

If you already learned how to relax, now it's time to start the practice of meditation to master stress.

Here are three meditations I can most emphatically recommend:

Return to the Womb

Sit comfortably. Relax.

Close your eyes.

Start to go back in time. Remember, for example, how you were a year ago. Then remember how you were three to five years ago. Keep going back in time, because the purpose is for you to start living retrospectively until remembering exactly, or as accurately as possible, how you were when you were a child. If you don't succeed in remembering, then imagine it.

Imagine now that you are in your mother's womb. Visualize yourself like that, small, in a fetal position. Feel as happy as you were then, free of all worries and concerns. At this time, nothing is more important than this sense of well-being, than this warm sensation of peace that surrounds you.

Enjoy this peace and well-being for as long as possible.

Sun and Surf

Close your eyes. Relax.

Try to remember a beach. You walk on the sand barefooted until you finally reach the shore.

Now the waves cover your feet. You walk a little further, going into the sea because you realize that the pleasant caressing water, now reaching up to your calves, has the magical quality of being able to extract from your body any kind of negative energy.

The sky is a cloudless blue and the rays of the sun shine down warmly on you.

Feel the warmth of the sun. Experience the sensation that the sunshine, upon passing through the center of your head, fills you with positive energy.

Experience the two sensations at once: the positive energy passing through the center of your head and providing you with vitality, and the negative energy from any affliction, illness, or concern, leaving your body through your feet and being carried away by the sea.

A Special Place

Visualize a place where you felt very happy once, where you felt the absolute notion of inner peace. It might be a forest, a beach, or a room in your house.

Think that in that place no worry or concern can touch you. Now there is nothing more important for you to do than enjoy the peace that this place affords you.

Perhaps, all of a sudden, you might get the idea that you're losing the battle because, unexpectedly and unintentionally, the memory of some worry, of something that you think you should have done differently, pops into your mind.

Don't make any effort to wipe this concern from your mind. Accept it. Even be grateful it appeared because, you now have an effective method to prevent this concern from appearing again in the future and causing unease.

Mentally transform this source of concern, for example, into a cigarette. Light a match. Watch its flame. Apply the flame to the tip of the cigarette. Watch it burn. Watch how it keeps burning, how it consumes itself as the smoke rises until it is lost in the distance.

When the cigarette disappears completely, when not even ashes are left, peace will come back to you. Enjoy it. Remember that inner peace means health.

Part V

Health and Longevity

*The ultimate purpose of health care
is universal vitality:
the prevention of aging,
the liberation of the mind from negativity,
and the achievement of spiritual enlightenment.*

—Ryokyu Endo

*The body and the energy system
are naturally
geared toward health.*

—Barbara Ann Brennan

So much has been written and discussed during the past few years about longevity and aging that not only scientists but an infinite number of people understand how we age: a loss of muscle and skeletal mass takes place, cholesterol and blood-pressure levels increase with a resulting risk of cardiovascular disease, arteries harden, wrinkles appear due to collagen alterations, and cellular mutations accumulate that give rise to malignant tumors that kill one out of every three persons over seventy years of age.

Though we already know *how* we age, on the other hand no one has been able to explain precisely *why* it is we age. Up to this moment science has not advanced a valid

71

reason to accept the inevitability of aging. Lab experiments have been performed that apparently explain this fact: the normal cells of a fetus, cultured in optimum conditions, divide fifty times before they die, while the cells of older individuals, who are apparently approaching the "Hayflick limit, " divide only between two and ten times and then they die. Such experiments may lead us to think that indeed cells undergo changes as they age and, therefore, aging and death have been built into the design of each one of us from the very moment of birth.

However, numerous other lab experiments proved that some abnormal cells, among them cancer cells, also cultured under optimum conditions, continue dividing indefinitely. Here's a mystery that science has not yet been able to explain: the reason why normal cells lose their capacity for proliferation. We should not blindly accept the theory, so popular today, that free radicals are responsible for human aging since the organism, in trying to maintain an equilibrium, at the same time produces antioxidant enzymes that counteract the harmful effects of free radicals. While genetic engineering keeps working to create immortal cells, the most viable method to prevent aging would be to find a way to ensure on a permanent basis the equilibrium programmed by cellular intelligence.

The function of ensuring this inner equilibrium or harmony falls exclusively under the purview of the human mind. Sankara, one of the great Indian thinkers, pointed out that people die only because previously they have seen others age and die. We have been conditioned to the idea, generation after generation, that around the age of fifty or before our decline will start and, therefore, we have no other option but to learn to age gracefully, to accept with resignation that with each passing day our health will be more precarious, and that we'll be closer to the day we will cease to exist. In reality we age, or rather age before our time, only because we are controlled by this way of thinking.

If we could have a new point of view, if we could accept the notion that in the ultimate analysis we are energy and not solid matter, if our mind were capable of sending vitality information to each organ in our body, if we could live above and beyond any affliction, as Buddha preached, if we were able to prevent the damage caused by the pressures of modern living, if it were possible to wipe away stress (which of course we can, thanks to meditation, among other techniques), if we could hold on to the belief that we human beings are the only ones that are able to change our biology through the thoughts and feelings we experience—then we would achieve the miracle of preserving youth possibly beyond one hundred years of age.

Many studies support the idea that people program their own aging. In his book *Exploring the Human Aura: A New Way of Viewing and Investigating Psychic Phenomena* (Prentice-Hall, 1975), Nicholas M. Regush, after stating that the metabolic process steadily and progressively slows down from birth to old age, then expresses the opinion that the problem may lie in the fact that we see this process as inevitable. As the basis for that opinion, Regush mentions the example of people who can walk on fire without getting burned, an ability developed through a ritual passed on from generation to generation in Algeria, India, Sri Lankha, Fiji, Japan, and Malaysia. These peoples have engaged in sustaining this logic-defying behavior not only because they think that they are protected by a divine power, but also because they respond to cultural patterns that enable them to acquire absolute control over their bodies and minds.

In *Beyond Telepathy* (Doubleday, 1973), Andrija Puh-arich says that mucous membranes are covered by moisture and that this "secretion is regulated mainly by the cholinergic system." It is a known fact that cholinergy may be defined as a state of relaxation and well-being characterized by the activation of the parasympathetic nervous system. So if mental control makes it possible to perform the impossible—why won't new mental patterns be able to overcome what until now seems impossible, i.e., to prevent the breakdown caused by the passage of time?

According to Buffon's biological curves, human beings, as happens with any other mammal, are expected to live sixfold the time it takes them to complete their growth. Hence human existence should last at least to 100 or 120. If this does not happen, there must be a reason that will explain it, perhaps the reason pointed out by San-kara: because we *think* it is impossible to reach 100.

Ayurveda, the thousands-of-years-old medical science of India and Tibet, deems it as fact that we can revert the aging process by means of the "five rituals," that is, the five breathing exercises, which are as easy to practice as Yoga exercises. In his book *Ancient Secrets of the Fountain of Youth* (Harbor Press, Inc., 1989), Peter Kelder relates meeting many elderly individuals who practiced these rites and were able to regain their youthful appearance. The explanation may be simple: whoever does these five exercises will manage to balance, store, and regenerate in his body the vital force that Hindus call *prana* and Tibetans *lung*. The Ayurveda medical system tirelessly teaches that lung is what keeps the body youthful and healthy.

These five rites are found in what we call today preventive med-icine, and popular lore has even coined a proverb that expresses its meaning: an ounce of prevention is better than a pound of cure. To prevent disease, however, you don't have to use pharmacological means. There are other methods that range from acupuncture and homeopathy to chronobiology, from shiatsu, iridology, and prayer, to diet plans, from meditation to aerobic exercises. The prevention of disease, locating it before it starts to create havoc in the organ-ism, can be achieved through esoteric means.

Tibetan astrology, for example, considers *newas*, i.e., birth marks, to be very important, as they are used to discover a person's physi-cal, psychological and spiritual predispositions. Each year is gov-erned by a newa and the newa for the year in which a person is born exerts a powerful influence over all aspects of that person's life, her or his health included.

This point of view has led us to think that medical astrology might be an effective method to discover the diseases we are prone to, so that we can start taking in time the medications needed to pre-vent those pathologies and keep our good health. A birth card, therefore, is full of revealing signs, each of which indicates the path and perhaps even the exact moment an illness might surprise us if we are not proactive enough and do not pay close attention to the message from the stars.

In a very schematic, summarized fashion let's review the close relation between zodiacal signs and the various parts of the body: Aries rules the head, Taurus the throat, Gemini the arms and lungs, Cancer the thymus and the digestive system, Leo the heart, Virgo the gastrointestinal system, Libra the kidneys, Scorpio the reproductive organs, Sagittarius the large femoral arteries, Capricorn the knees, Aquarius the calves, and Pisces the feet.

Without pretending that he or she is making a medical diagnosis, and only for purposes of warning the patient, the astrologist explains in more detail the examination and reveals with amazing accuracy any predisposition to disease—for example, a conjunction of Jupiter and Saturn may foretell digestive system disorders, or that one is more prone to develop diabetes if the birth card shows a conjunction of Jupiter with Uranus, a combination which, by the way, endows those born on that date with generosity and with an inclination toward studying the occult.

Should anyone not hold the predictions of medical astrology in high regard, that person must at least accept one thing that has been verified and proven: that thoughts and feelings change cellular biochemistry. When we are overwhelmed by pain or fear, hormones are secreted that send messages to various parts of the body. The same thing occurs when we feel love, happiness, or compassion for others, the only difference being that when we have happy feelings, these feelings foster health, whereas anger or hate unleash neurotransmitters that cause the opposite effect, i.e., produce physiological changes that immediately affect blood pressure and the immune system negatively, and subsequently engender pathological conditions.

Our body is the result and sum total of everything we think and feel, not of the events per se (a car accident, being imprisoned, the death of a loved one), but the interpretation we make of those events that impact our lives. Contrary to what has been assumed, the human brain does not register the images of reality like a mirror, but rather examines and interprets that reality. Maintaining a certain healthy state is conditioned by the interpretations we have learned to make since childhood, which were instilled when we were born, or even long before when the sperm fertilized the egg, and our mother started to transmit information to each molecule of our genetic code. The fear of such a harmless creature as a frog, for example, could have been transmitted subconsciously by my mother, without her being aware of such transfer. The fear inspired by thunder and lightning could have been instilled into my subconscious by an aunt who, sitting next to my cradle when I was two months old, constantly made the sign of the cross thinking that she would thus keep away the dangers of an electrical storm.

All of these interpretations impacting the physical body, as a whole, will predispose us to health or disease. The well-directed mind can become an adequate tool to preserve and promote health. With such a mind we can influence our heart rate, our body temperature, and the thresholds of pain and pleasure. But most people don't know how to start their own mental mechanism through which they control essential aspects of their lives.

Falling ill, growing old, enjoying good health—all of these possibilities are under the control of our mental body, but the mental body cannot exert a rigid control over the emotional body. "When will and imagination are in conflict, imagination will always win out," said the French hypnotist and chemist Emile Coué. From this it follows that if a person consumes his or her psychic energy by insisting on thinking of a feeling that person wants to wipe from his or her mind, usually the opposite happens, and such a mental attitude precisely strengthens that feeling. Feelings, emotions, energy, and physics teach us that energy cannot be destroyed but only transformed. We can change feelings of hate into love, and anger into compassion. If we are convinced that the interpretation of events affect us more than the events themselves, then we can transform a feeling of anguish into an opposite emotion.

We can start this fascinating alchemic process immediately, or as soon as we want to. It doesn't matter if we have been struggling in vain against a feeling of hate for months or years. If we lose the battle, it is because we chose the wrong way to defeat it.

Mental Alchemy

Through meditation the emotional body can start to let go the feelings of guilt, fear, or hate, just like a tree lets go of its leaves in fall and winter, not as a sign of death and permanent dissolution, but rather of transformation—like a promise of the greenness that will return to its branches. We must let go of our negative emotions just like the tree lets go of its dry leaves, because emotions are processed in the belly area, in the manipura or solar plexus chakra, where they trigger multiple reactions that in turn decisively affect the physical body. As one more evidence of Oriental wisdom, in ancient Japan they often talked of "disciplining the abdomen" as a means to achieve the mind-body connection and storing energy in the *tanden* area of the belly—an effective strategy to prevent the progression of a disease.

There are numerous techniques that make it possible to produce the mental alchemy indispensable for health. The Ayurveda system teaches that intention plays an important role in generating the benefits we can obtain from any healing technique, whether it be aromatherapy, hydrotherapy, or essential-oil massage. Hence the fantastic results obtained by positive affirmations.

It suffices that we decide to formulate these affirmations for the intention to be transformed into action, a concept that is becoming more and more fashionable these days, as science begins to understand the mind-body relationship and the connections between spirituality and health, as if our own genetic code were programmed to make us believe in a higher power and to let us know that by just changing our behavior, by being filled with faith and optimism, we can overcome any disease and prolong our useful life.

Many studies have revealed that prayer has positive effects in the healing of many illnesses, and that people who have meditated regularly for some time exhibit a younger biological age than their actual chronological one, which shows that meditation can stop the aging process and even revert it. It is also known that through visualization and directed-imaging therapies we can activate the body's defenses and repair the physical body. Physicians are not unaware of

these "miraculous" cures—they themselves have seen numerous re-
missions, and have witnessed the spontaneous cures Dr. Weil talked
about. These are the reasons, and not any other, why every day an
ever-greater number of people decide to explore new or ancient
ways to increase our inner resistance to disease by specifically invoking the power of the mind.

Cellular Intelligence

There is a truth open to everyone: if positive affirmations or visualization techniques are used during meditation, they will increase to
the utmost your therapeutic potential because it can be activated in
the deepest layers of your self, a place inaccessible so far, to which
only meditation will open the door, a space full of peace and light
where the body's chemistry is generated, where cellular intelligence
resides, where the mind-body connection takes place, and where
psyche and soma join hands.

Chromotherapy and Meditation

Everything seems to indicate that the inhabitants of the disappeared
continent of Atlantis were the first to use color in diagnosing and
treating disease, a knowledge appropriated by the Egyptians, since
it is a known fact they already practiced it in 2500 B.C. Perhaps the
Indian art of healing known as Aryuveda had arisen long before. In
this method, chromotherapy becomes especially important, combined with aromatherapy, infusions, and essential-oil massages,
among other methods intended to foster bodily health.

Chromotherapy has always awakened interest. The physician
and philosopher Avicena, who lived until 1037, stated in his *Canon
of Medicine* that color was not only a guide to diagnosis but an effective remedy against any illness, an opinion also shared by the most
famous physician of antiquity, Paracelsus, and later on adopted by
Franz Anton Mesmer, the German physician who originated the
theory of healing through magnetism.

After a long period during which the interest in chromotherapy
waned, S. Pancoast's book *Blue and Red Light* (Stoddart, 1877)

appeared, describing the healing properties of these lights, and the next year *The Principles of Light and Color,** written and originally published by the physician Edwin Babbitt, developed healing systems that use colored glasses. Theosophists Charles Leadbeater and Annie Besant wrote exhaustively about the colors assumed by our thoughts, and in 1903 the Danish physician Niels Finsen received the Nobel Prize for his discovery of the healing effect of light and ultraviolet rays on several skin diseases. In 1937 *The Origin and Properties of the Human Aura* (University Books) was published by Dr. Oscar Bagnall, a Cambridge biologist, who was the first to explain that the colors of the aura were perceived by the rods in the eye's receptive field.

Semyon Davidovich Kirlian was the first person to successfully photograph the human aura, in 1939. Kirlian was born in Ekaterinodar, then a small town in southern Russia that after the Russian Revolution was renamed Krasnodar. Until the age of forty nothing foretold a brilliant future for Kirlian; he had not even completed high school and the only occupation in which he showed some ability was as an electrical engineer.

He became so skillful in his trade that his services were always in demand whenever any hospital electrical equipment broke down, whether a massage machine or an x-ray device. He was soon assigned the maintenance of all medical facilities in Krasnodar. Thanks to the financial security afforded by his new job, he decided to do what he had been longing to do for months—marry Valentina, a woman as exceptional as he was, who worked as a literature teacher in a high school and who, perhaps motivated not only by her love for Kirlian but by the passion she felt for photography, devotedly collaborated in all of her husband's experiments until her premature death in 1971, the victim of a strange and painful disease caused by too frequent exposure to high-voltage electrical current.

On one occasion a high-frequency Tesla generator broke down and since the hospital decided to get rid of it, Kirlian took it home to his tiny quarters at the intersection of Gorki and Kirov Streets and finally, after talking it over with Valentina, installed it in their own bedroom. It was not difficult to get it working again, after

---

* Republished in 1980 by Carol Publishing Group.

making the spare parts himself. From that moment on, according to Kirlian's own confession, any event good or bad that came his way was related to a high-frequency generator—sad events, such as the death of Valentina years later; happy events, such as when something happened that no one could have imagined as he repaired a high-frequency generator. Later on Kirlian related the event in these words: "I had had a scratch on my hand, and even though it had healed and there was no visible sign of it, I realized that in the high-intensity field around the generator you could see the scratch amazingly clearly."

Trying to understand the mystery, Kirlian decided to take a picture of his own hand by using the Tesla generator and a photographic film. The operation was simple: placing his hand on the electrode and briefly activating the generator. Valentina developed it immediately and before her eyes something appeared that resembled a radiograph, but wasn't quite one—it was the silhouette of the hand, with the bones neatly demarcated, but the unusual thing about the photo was the impressive halo that scintillated around the fingers. That night, according to Kirlian's account, neither Valentina nor he were able to sleep, rightly thinking that they had succeeded in recording on film for the first time the energy or vibration that quickens all living things, which till then only mystics and the founders of the great religions had talked about.

Kirlian also related that after taking the first photo of the aura, he and Valentina were so excited with the experiments that, almost in the frenzy of a sudden attack of madness, they took pictures of each other's auras almost daily, and that's how they discovered that their auras had a different color: Valentina's was surrounded by an orange radiance while Kirlian's aura was light blue. Later they showed that each person irradiated a different aura color and that these colors could vary depending on the emotions they were feeling at the time. Thanks to the discoveries by Kirlian and Valentina, nowadays we can record the human energy field on a Polaroid picture, whose colors will tell us whether that person is depressed or is overwhelmed by sexual desire or resentment. Another discovery by the Kirlians is that the different parts of the human body show different colors.

These various colors registered by the Kirlian camera match the seven main centers of energy or chakras, which have so much to do with our health and our spiritual growth.

The **first chakra**, or root chakra, also known as muladhara, is located at the base of the spine and is related to our basic survival mechanisms. A disorder in this chakra can cause bone cancer, leukemia and, in most cases, lack of vitality. The color of the first chakra is red.

The **second chakra**, called svadisthana, is located under the navel and is related to the liver, the belly, and the intestines. Its color is orange.

The **third chakra** or solar plexus chakra, located at the base of the sternum, is related to the emotional life. A disorder in this chakra can cause diabetes, ulcers, or hepatitis. It has a yellow color.

The **fourth chakra** or heart chakra is the chakra through which we love. This is where the energies from the terrestrial plane are transformed into spiritual energy through compassion and love. Its color is green, which from the psychological point of view symbolizes spring. All chromotherapists agree that the color green stimulates the regeneration of damaged tissues.

The **fifth** or throat chakra is the chakra for communication. According to Leadbeater this chakra confers the faculty of hearing on an astral plane. Its color is blue, the most healing of all colors.

The **sixth chakra**, called ajna, also known as the third eye because it is the center of intuition, is located between the eyebrows and is related to the pituitary gland or hypophysis, which coordinates the endocrine system. Many researchers link this gland to the internal clock of our body, so the phenomenon of aging is linked to the workings of the hypophysis and therefore to the energy flow through this chakra. Its color is indigo.

The **seventh chakra** or Chakra of a Thousand Petals is located in the upper part of the head and makes communication with cosmic energy possible, so by activating it an individual may attain wisdom and spiritual enlightenment. Its color is either magenta or white.

Chromatotherapy postulates that to heal an organ located in the area under the influence of a chakra, the color corresponding to that chakra must be projected on to that location. Many chromatotherapists recommend, without doing away with a physician but rather as an alternative therapy only, that we should have color filters in our homes, which turn out to be very effective in healing numerous diseases.

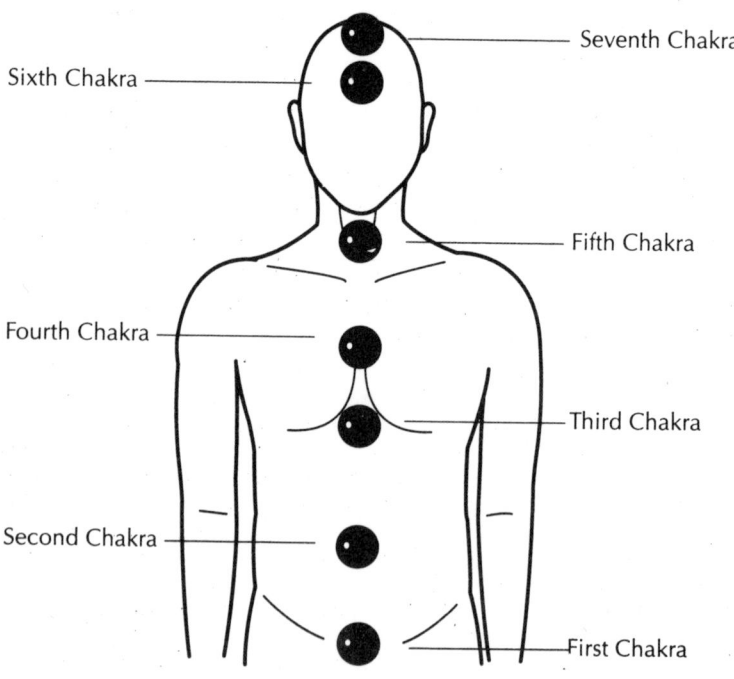

The Chakra System

Long-practicing meditators know that it is also possible to project the color mentally on to a certain area of the body with the same healing purpose. How do they do it? After sitting comfortably for one or two minutes on a chair or cushion, with the eyes closed, meditators start to repeat, as if it were a mantra, the name of the color they need to project.

After another one or two minutes, they see that as they repeat the name of the color it becomes progressively easier for them to visualize and therefore to direct it to the affected area. In the meditator's imagination the color may take on the characteristics of a flame that "burns" the impurities accumulated there. If you decide to perform this type of meditation, accept the visualization of the flame as one of the most ideal ways to achieve healing.

The color blue corresponds to the area of the neck and the upper area of the lungs. That is why, in cases of bronchitis, breast cancer, emphysema, and stiff neck, the meditator should mentally project the color blue on to the affected area.

Green corresponds to the chest and lower area of the lungs. It should be projected mentally during meditation in cases of chest angina, indigestion, or nausea.

Yellow corresponds to the solar plexus, the area that stores emotions, and should be projected in cases of depression and of skin conditions, whereas red is advisable for genital disorder cases.

The Skylight

Sit comfortably, half-close your eyes, and breathe deeply and slowly.

Pronounce your favorite mantra.

Now imagine that there is a skylight that sheds a powerful light in the room where you're meditating.

Allow that stream of white light to penetrate the center of your head, flooding your entire body and all the cells in your tissues.

Allow that white light to illuminate your internal universe.

If you are suffering from any bodily illness, you must visualize the color corresponding to the chakra that is next to that area of the body.

Let the healing color do its work.

Before completing your meditation, focus again on your breathing rhythm. Breathe deeply and slowly. Then return to normal respiration.

Repeat mentally: "I feel perfectly all right."

Origin of Disease

A continuous circulation of energy prevails in a healthy body. Ancient Chinese medicine discovered that energy circulates along invisible meridians that traverse the while body from head to toe and establishes a direct relation with the various organs. To simplify this concept, we could say that energy circulates through the meridians (which the Chinese call *jing*, meaning "conduit") in the same way blood circulates through veins and arteries.

Western medicine has refused to accept the existence of meridians since these ducts, which are the very essence of life, can't be found when an autopsy is performed—they disappear at the moment of death. However, it cannot be denied that when a needle is passed through any of the acupuncture points, of which there are close to a thousand, the normal circulation of energy is reestablished in that meridian, which is of course located at the same place as the diseased organ. The practice of acupuncture has proved it: reestablishing the free flow of energy reestablishes health. Thoughts and feelings are expressions of energy. When our mind grows gloomier because of negative thoughts or feelings, the flow of energy becomes disorganized, causing an unbalance in the energy guidelines that run through the body, at times producing a deficit or an excess of energy in a certain area. Illness is caused by either a lack or an overabundance of energy around a specific organ, since both situations prevent the harmonious flow of energy in our internal world.

Those who are able to see the unseen world are convinced that health is not only a personal responsibility—it is also a cosmic obligation because our disharmony will reflect negatively on the free flow along the energy guidelines of the universe. Hence the whole body of oriental medicine (from Aryuveda to Shiatsu) postulates that a diseased condition takes hold when a person loses internal harmony and therefore interrupts the exchange of information with universal energy.

A scientist could say the same thing today in other words: human beings succumb to disease when they lose control of their consciousness. In the Western world very few will deny that the mind plays an essential role in causing disease, whether it be high blood pressure, depression, or heart conditions, which oftentimes are as deadly as cancer. When we experience a certain feeling, hormones are secreted that in turn cause changes in our metabolism and physiology. We ought to emphasize this again: if the feelings involve love, compassion, friendship, and altruism, the physiological changes that take place will turn into good health, whereas gloomy thoughts and feelings of anger, fear, or resentment will cause changes in body chemistry that will unleash opposite physiological processes.

The body reveals, through its healthy or diseased state, the language of our subconscious. That is, the mind uses the body to express the feelings of anger, hate, or frustration that we have been storing within. It uses the body to transmit a message that would otherwise remain hidden. That is why the unbalanced condition starts somewhere in our psyche before emerging at the physical level, i.e., before becoming a psychosomatic illness. All or almost all diseases share this cause. Throat conditions, for example, reflect a refusal to accept life's demands. When we say we can't quite swallow an idea, this means that we don't accept it. Here's a healing meditation advisable for this type of disease:

> Visualize all the pleasant things that life affords us: the love for our mate, for our parents, for our children, Nature in all its splendor, works of art that give us great esthetic pleasure.

In the course of this meditation repeat mentally or aloud the Zen teaching: "If we don't learn to appreciate the mystery and beauty of our life and of our present time, we shall never appreciate the value of any life at any time."

A peptic ulcer reflects feelings of aggression or fear. Internal conflicts are stored in the solar plexus, giving rise to disorders such as indigestion or heartburn. Recommended meditation:

Visualize yourself traveling on a cloud, over buildings, valleys, mountains, and the sea. Feel that you are flying away from conflicts, which at that height cannot affect you.

Asthma expresses the need to receive. It appears when a person feels the need to be accepted, acknowledged, and loved by others. Recommended meditation:

Visualize yourself as a success. Relive events in which people (your relatives, acquaintances, and friends) looked up to you and admired you.

The skin is the border with the outer world. Skin conditions reflect fears and insecurities of which we are not aware.

Meditation

Visualize your whole body covered by metal plating. Imagine how, little by little, your body starts to be covered by gold, silver, or bronze plating. First your feet, calves, and thighs, and then your belly, arms, neck, and head. You should feel the sensation that the plating affixed to your skin becomes an armor that, at the same time it protects you, confers an air of authority upon you.

Cancer reflects a sustained feeling of frustration or resentment as well as a tendency to love other people more than oneself. Recommended meditation:

Visualize an energy consisting of the purest love running through your body, illuminating the darkest zones of your inner world.

Risotherapy (Laughter Therapy)

When we fall ill, the first thing we feel is fear. We suddenly experience that our life is threatened. We may think, to a certain extent not without reason, that the disease in question may bring about our death. Any illness may hold this peril. As soon as pain appears, we start becoming afraid of the future, aware that each new day our health will grow much weaker.

Fear, in short, is nothing but the loss of hope. And hope, no need to say it, means on the contrary the desire to attain a future in which everything that is dark will turn to light, in which faith can work the miracle of returning us to our previous state of health. It will be impossible to recover our well-being, for as long as we are unable to experience complete confidence that recovering our health is perfectly possible. All physicians have seen for themselves that the patients that heal soonest are those who have faith in their treatments, who look at the future with enthusiasm and constantly are setting new goals for themselves.

The opposite feeling to fear is not happiness but optimism. When experiencing a tragedy it is permissible and logical to feel sad, but without this sad state persisting, becoming depression, and leading us to think that nothing good awaits us in life. To foster optimism the best remedy and resource is laughter. *Risotherapy*, also known as laughter therapy, is a recently coined term, but it is gaining more and more acceptance, especially since the experiences of Steven Sultanoff, past president of the Association for Applied and Therapeutic Humor, and of Robert Holden, founder of the first laughter clinic in Great Britain.

The health benefits derived from funny films are immeasurable. Charlie Chaplin, Buster Keaton, the Marx brothers, Fernandel, Cantinflas, Woody Allen, Dustin Hoffman, and Whoopi Goldberg have made a great contribution to the health of so many people. The scene in *Annie Hall* in which Woody Allen and Diane Keaton are afraid of throwing a live lobster in boiling water, which finally ends up in the pot, causing them to feel guilty of homicide, initiated in all movie-watchers what we would call today laughter therapy. Below you will find a recommended meditation:

Reviving Mirth

Close your eyes. Relax.

Remember an occasion in which you had what you could call an irresistible laughter attack.

Now you are going to relive it.

Breathe deeply and slowly. When you complete the third breath, try to remember in detail that instant in which you were taken over by an episode of laughter.

Look at yourself from the outside, as if you were looking at someone else laughing.

Without striving to make an effort, allow all the details of that joyful scene to flood your memory as if you traveled smoothly through time until arriving at that "there and then."

Listen to your laughter. Try to hear it as precisely as possible as the laughter penetrates you, shakes you from the inside and comes out of your own mouth.

Be as happy as you were then. Be that happy as long as your concentration allows.

Healing Through the Five Elements

Ancient Chinese wisdom taught the presence of the five elements that make up all natural phenomena and that, if we accept the close relationship between the Macrocosmos and the Microcosmos, we can also apply them to the human body. Those five elements are: wood, fire, earth, water, and metal.

Each of these elements is directly related to one or several organs in our body: wood to the liver, fire to the heart, earth to the belly, metal to the lungs, and water to the kidneys. During meditation we can make use of those five elements to improve our bodily health.

People with some kind of liver condition may perform the following meditation:

Close your eyes. Relax.

Breathe deeply and slowly, directing the air to your belly, just as you would have done if you had performed "full respiration."

Imagine that this air, now transformed into energy, passes through the trunks of high, strong trees or large heaps of wood, and immediately thereafter visualize this energy, charged up in turn by the wood's energy, reaching your liver and cleansing it of all the impurities that cause your illness.

If you suffer from any belly ailment, start your meditation just as in the previous one, but this time imagining the following:

A mass of energy springs forth from the earth and reaches your belly, causing it to heal.

If you suffer from a lung disease, you should start the meditation with the following visualization:

A mass of energy coming from some metal performs a healing action in your lungs. Afterward, imagine that your lungs are lined with metal plating (gold, silver, or any other metal) in order to protect them from any other disease.

If a person suffers from a kidney disease, that individual should start to meditate by imagining the following:

The air you breathe in takes on the properties of water inside your body. Water is a fluid element with an enormous mystical power, both physically and spiritually.

Imagine that the air you have breathed in has turned into water, a water that cleanses your kidneys of all impurities and heals them.

If you have heart disease, perform the following meditation:

Imagine that the air you breathe while you meditate is transformed into love energy. Direct that energy to your heart as if it were a fire that burns all the impurities that cause the disease.

Think that as of that moment you will be a more loving, more altruistic and happier person.

How to Heal at a Distance

If you want to serve others, most particularly in the field of health, you must become convinced that everybody has that gift and that it is even possible to heal at a distance, without that individual realizing the help being given.

Go into the room that you have set aside for meditation and close the door. Sit comfortably and relax.

Visualize the person that you are going to heal, exploring all of his or her body from head to toe. A moment will come at which an area of that person's body will cause you to stop the exploration. Concentrate on that area.

Use your hands to "sweep" with vigorous gestures any negative energy stored in that part of the body.

Imagine that the negative energy, as you "sweep it" with your hands, falls to the floor and gets lost in the deepest reaches of the Earth, where it can't harm anyone. Now focus powerful beams of healing light on the affected area.

You should always start with a powerful beam of white light and then apply the light appropriate to the area of the body you're healing.

Thank the Supreme Being for the opportunity of being able to help another human being.

Learning to Close Up

Even though psychotronics asserts that energy is not transferable, several Japanese scientists were able to use devices to control the acupuncture process in order to study the energy exchanges that take place between healer and patient in the course of spiritual healing. These studies determined that at the end of the session the healer's energy readings showed an imbalance while the patient's showed an increase in vital energy.

Even though theoretically energy cannot be transferred, the feeling of compassion is so strong that the healer may share part of his energy with the patient. That is why if someone uses meditation to heal another individual, the healer needs to learn to close up. Closing up in this case means protecting oneself, because the energy imbalance that may take place is not the only risk assumed by the healer.

When you're trying to heal someone else, what you're doing is separating from that person's body the negative energy that had accumulated in a certain area of his or her body. It often happens that the healer becomes impregnated with some residues of that negative energy, with ensuing risk of falling sick or feeling indisposed for several days.

To prevent this, as soon as you finish a healing effort, you must visualize a powerful flame that will burn all the impurities that had remained around the patient. Then visualize a circle of light. Place yourself inside this circle, confident of the fact that it will be your best protection.

Part VI

The House of Health

What it counts as joy is health.

—Thomas Merton

Up to now we have described what we could say is passive meditation. We adopt an appropriate posture, with our back upright, eyes half-closed and hands on our laps, the palm of the right hand on the palm of the left hand. We focus all our attention on our breathing rhythm, trying to prolong the pauses between breathing in and out because we are aware that the slower this rhythm, the greater the benefits our body will reap during and after the meditation. We start by pronouncing one word, a mantra, perhaps OM, the primordial sound, to promote an ever-deeper state of relaxation. Then we let go, we let ourselves be carried away because we have not the slightest doubt that someone is leading us by the hand to the deepest reaches of our biological nature, down to unsuspected levels of awareness, at the end of which the encounter with the Absolute is to take place. During such an encounter we'll perceive somehow, in a state of ecstasy, that the core of energy power that is the kundalini, which seemed to be dormant, stored in the perineum (the coiled snake biting its tail), suddenly awakens and starts to go up from the coccyx, throughout the length of the whole spine, proceeding through the whole system of chakras until reaching the pineal gland and rushing forth as a stream of light through the exact center of the head.

Before our awareness has reached this level of expansion and we are invaded by the fragrance of this unique experience, before attaining the "Pursued Light," the meditator can and should experiment with his or her own lights, those that he can create at will for the most diverse ends: to keep his internal balance, to perceive bodily rhythms, to discipline the mind, to shed light on areas of our unconscious life that lie in wait in the dense darkness of emotions that once caused us tears and suffering, or anger and hatred that we've not been able to get rid of, or to shed light on the spaces occupied within us by the masters of all religions, where the inner Christ reigns that Saint Paul talked about. Using these lights created by

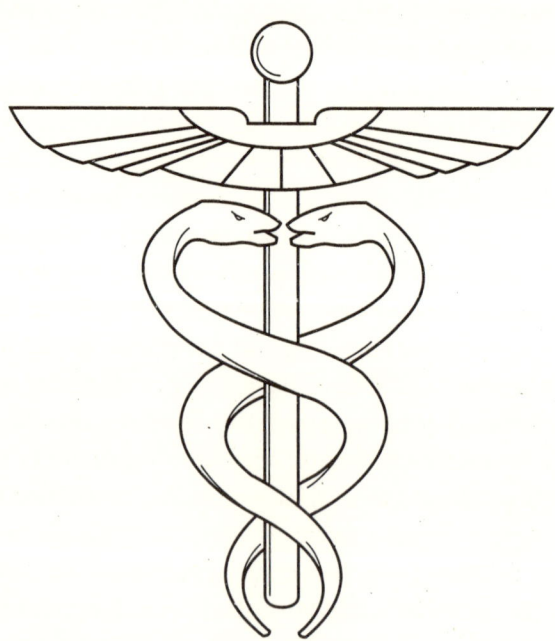

Kundalini

ourselves is a way of performing an active or directed meditation. We can't rely on anyone, as Buddha advised. We are a lamp unto ourselves.

Taking Advantage of the Biorhythm

The behavior of human biological energy rhythms has been the subject of study since the most ancient times. In 1593, André Laurens explained in *De crisbus* that every disease reaches its worst point on the seventh day and its conclusion on the twenty-first. Roch le Baillif pointed out that human cycles are multiples of seven, an idea shared by Malfatti who said that "the four ages of man unfold as a function of the multiplication of three times seven: twenty-one years old (youth), forty-two years old (virility), sixty-three years old (old age), and eighty-four years old (decrepitude)."

In ancient Egypt, as well as in Syria, Persia, and Macedonia, there were physician-priests, Hippocrates among them, who were called in Greek *periodeutas*, by virtue of their knowledge about body rhythms, which they used to heal many illnesses.

Numerous studies seem to confirm that cancer is a disease whose appearance and development is influenced by body rhythms, since it usually takes its toll at the ages of forty-two, forty-nine, fifty-six, and sixty-three. Dr. Krumm-Heller, in his book *Biorhythm* says that this seven-year cycle becomes evident in women as well, because if they give birth at the age of twenty-one, twenty-eight or thirty-five, the child will bear an exact resemblance to the mother. Another interesting case mentioned by Krumm-Heller is that of Tolstoy, who was born on August 28, 1828. Krumm-Heller was able to ascertain that most major events in his life always took place on the twenty-eighth day of a month.

Dr. Franz Halberg, professor of medicine at the University of Minnesota, founder of a new science called Chronobiology, has talked at length about the need to get back in step with our biological rhythms in order to achieve internal equilibrium on which our health depends. To Dr. Halberg, living in harmony with these biorhythms is to listen to the "body's music," i.e., paying attention to the messages coming from the mind-body system, some of which are common to all human beings. Chronobiologists have deciphered these messages: in the morning our capacity to pay attention increases, short-term memory functions fully, and sexual relations are most satisfying; around noon body temperature increases and sight is sharpest; in the course of the afternoon manual dexterity peaks, and when night falls our metabolism is at its lowest point.

Half a century before, Dr. Milton Erickson, founder of the American Society of Clinical Hypnosis, noticed in the course of his practice as a hypnotherapist that every so often certain changes took place in the receptive state of the minds of his patients, during which hypnotic suggestions to promote healing found a more fertile ground, which also led him to think that the body spontaneously was cooperating in its own healing. His many years of experience taught Erickson that those periods, which made it easier for him to reach the subconscious, lasted from ten to twenty minutes.

Subsequently, French neurologist Jean-Martin Charcot stressed that people experience several times a day a state of consciousness intermediate between sleep and wakefulness, which he called the hypnoidal state. Pierre Janet, one of his disciples, insisted that these "pauses in the course of the day" were related to physical exhaustion and that precisely during those periods the body was able to get back its lost energies. These spontaneous changes in the states of consciousness were also pointed out by Freud and Jung, but it wasn't until the 1950s that scientists, thanks to scientific breakthroughs, started to detect the internal rhythms of rest and activity that lasted from ninety to one hundred twenty minutes. Such circadian-ultradian rhythms corroborated the notion theorized by Milton Erickson that every so often the body needs to pause in order to regenerate itself.

Now we know that most of the time a cellular renewal is taking place in the body, but also that during each one of those pauses programmed by biorhythm, lasting twenty minutes, a holistic healing response ensues when the repair system of the body becomes activated. These healing responses must be taken advantage of in performing any of the techniques used for therapeutic purposes, whether it be meditation, hypnosis, psychotronics, biofeedback, bioenergotherapy, visualization, and even religious expressions such as shamanism, Mary Baker Eddy's Christian Science, tantric healing, or the imposition of hands as practiced, among others, by the followers of Allan Kardec.

Healing Meditation

Holistic healing, which approaches the patient as a whole, has received strong recognition in the past few years in some fields of medical science. Many oncologists think that it is possible that a cancerous tumor may appear in a person at the place of least organic resistance when that person's natural immunity becomes compromised, thus undermining his or her health. That is why no patient will be fully healed by receiving treatment for an individual organ since, against the opinion traditionally held by Western medicine, even if an illness appears to be circumscribed to a certain part of the body, in reality it is a generalized disease.

If medical technology is focused on the treatment of an individual organ, a cure may take place, but not healing, whose purpose is to give back to the whole body the health it previously enjoyed. In oriental wisdom a sick person is an individual who has interrupted his exchange of information with Cosmic Intelligence. Treatment must consist, therefore, in the patient's recovery of the ability to vibrate in harmony with nature and in having his or her Microcosmos identify itself again with the Macrocosmos by falling in tune again with the rhythm of the Universe.

When the great guru Padmasambhava arrived in Tibet to establish the Vajrayana School of Buddhism, also known as the Tantra Way, one of his first teachings had to do with the care and maintenance of health. He taught that true health is attained when we are able to create a source of happiness that will nourish our well-being and is useful to others. He taught the practice of meditation in order to deepen spiritual life and to establish a firm connection with bodily intelligence, that kind of magic that enables the body to repair itself. "I worked for my body's health while sitting on my heels," said Milarepa centuries later. This is what healing meditation is after: perfect health, which cannot be attained if we don't learn the art of concentrating, a direct way to hear the most subtle messages issued constantly by the body.

Tantric Self-Healing

Meditating is not just practicing relaxation. It is coming to a standstill so that our thoughts and feelings quiet down. It is sitting comfortably on a cushion or a chair, forgetting about the demands of the environment, focusing on a fixed point, perhaps on a small flame that flickers in the darkness. Meditating is also asking the Supreme Healers to grant the gift of health.

Tantric Self-Healing teaches us to meditate on the five Supreme Healers: Akshobya ("The one who sustains life"), who is blue and from his heart heals mental illness, high blood pressure, arthritis and intestinal problems; Amitabha, who is red and from the throat chakra heals lung and liver diseases; Vairochana, who is white and heals brain disorders as well as glandular diseases; Amo-ghasiddi, who is green, occupies the pubic region, and should be the subject of our meditations to heal sex disorders and constipation; and finally Ratnasambbhava, who is yellow, resides in the navel area, and to whose compassion we should appeal to heal kidney diseases and skin conditions.

How do you meditate to attain healing? If you remember the image of one of these Supreme Healers, you can evoke it while you meditate, reconstructing it in your imagination little by little until completing the full image. If these images are not familiar to you, you can reconstruct the image of Jesus or of Saint Lazarus, two great Master Healers who will come quickly to your aid. But no matter who is the Master of whom you ask favors, before even starting your request you ought to reflect on the purpose that motivated you to meditate, then you should visualize the image of the Healer, ask for permission to perform the meditation and finally humbly express your gratefulness for the grace conferred.

The Master Healer

Lida, my guardian angel, told me that there is a place called the House of Health, where we should migrate mentally during meditation to establish communication with the Master Healer. It is not a dwelling made with regular materials, such as those we are used to seeing, but rather a vegetable enclosure whose walls and ceiling may be the branches of luxuriant trees, and where the seats are bushes molded into the shape of a chair or sofa, perhaps through the expertise of a master pruner. On the floor we can find at our disposal, for the purpose of sitting down to meditate, numerous cushions made and stuffed with blades of grass that delight us with their fragrance and fresh greenness.

As soon as we enter the House of Health, a guru approaches us solicitously. He greets us by joining the palms of his hands at his chin and immediately explains to us the steps to follow:

First Step: we may sit on any *zafu*, or round cushion, of our choice, with our feet crossed so that the knees rest on the floor below the hip, or we may sit on a chair with our hands being supported by our knees.

Second Step: we should start breathing deeply and slowly, trying to prolong inhalation as much as possible while we push the air to the tanden area of the abdomen known as the "ocean of energy."

Third Step: each time you perform an inspiration, repeat the word OM or the mantra that first comes to your mind.

Fourth Step: focus all your attention on your breathing rhythm, appreciate how the air descends to the tanden area of the abdomen and leaves your body through your nostrils. When you inhale say "one," when you exhale say "two," when you inhale say "three," and so on until you reach twenty-one.

Fifth Step: start to visualize the image of the Master Healer, ask for his permission to perform your meditation, and implore his help to recover or to maintain good health.

Sixth Step: think that the Master Healer, who is located in front of you, is constantly sending you beams of light that spring from his chest, specifically from the place where his loving heart gleams. Watch how the beams of light issued by the Master Healer's heart enter your body through your nostril and purify it all. Breathe in that blue light issuing from the Master Healer for as long as possible.

Seventh Step: humbly and joyfully express your gratefulness both to the Master Healer and the guru who told you the steps to follow during meditation. Prior to standing up and leaving the House of Health, think that you don't want the benefits received only for yourself, but that they must be extended to your family members, to your friends, to your potential enemies and to the whole human race.

Buddhist teachings assert that dedicating the merits acquired to others is the same as pouring a drop of water into the ocean, but not doing so is to allow that drop to evaporate on the desert sand.

The Power to Heal

Hindus call it prana. Some people have called it the vital fluid. Others have named it the essential force, the creative force, vital magnetism while others have called it God's energy. These various names, any one of which you may accept, refer to the same thing: a unifying energy exists in the universe that promotes life and which, when it becomes individualized, enters the human body and at the same time wraps it and protects it.

This extrasensory perception band or etheric envelope, usually called astral aura or astral body, which according to Leadbeater may be full of vivid colors, is almost invisible at plain sight even though there are people who have been able to perceive it with ease, and it has even been photographed by Semyon and Valentina Kirlian, who used photographic film, together with a high-powered generator. As we have said, the health of a human being depends on the person's ability to absorb vital energy, to prevent damage to his or her magnetic field and to succeed in maintaining a harmonious energy flow through all parts of the body. If an imbalance disrupts that energy flow, disease ensues. This is why many have asserted that there are no diseases but sick people, that most illnesses are psychosomatic and that the power of the mind can guarantee our bodily health because the mind is specifically intended to preserve the harmony in that magnetic field that surrounds and to see that its envelope is not harmed. If a person, out of negligence, oversight, or ignorance, or any other reason, has not been able to protect and preserve his aura and suffers an illness, which is nothing but a hole through which vital energy leaks, then that person needs the aid of someone else to help seal that opening through which health escapes, and restore the harmony in that body, which up to that moment was afflicted by some disease.

From the most ancient times there have been people able to perform this restoring task. In Egypt, priests in the temples of Serapis, Isis, and Osiris laid on their hands to heal their patients. The same thing was done by Aesculapius, and more recently by the physician Franz Anton Mesmer. The idea has persisted throughout history that it is possible to heal the sick by the laying on of the hands.

Chapter 8 of the Gospel of Saint Matthew reads: "When he was come from the mountain, great multitudes followed him. And, behold, there came a leper and worshipped him, saying, 'Lord, if thou wilt, thou canst make me clean.' And Jesus put forth his hand, and touched him, saying, 'I will, be thou clean.' And immediately his leprosy was cleansed." In an attempt to rationalize (if that were possible) this miraculous cure, just as in many others performed by Jesus, we have to rely on the authority of Dr. Mesmer, who created the first method of healing through magnetism. Mesmer stressed that we all can become healers, that any person willing to serve a fellow human being could be charged "like a battery" with that vital energy and transmit it to the sick, using the hands as a conduit for the vital force so it could exert its beneficial effect in the body of the patient.

According to Mesmer, a healer must cleanse the body of the patient, just as perhaps Jesus himself did, by extracting the negative vibrations or energies stored somewhere in the body. If the healer is right-handed his or her positive hand is the right one, and if left-handed, the left hand. In order to extract those negative energies, the therapist should place the negative hand on the area of the body affected by the illness or pain while the positive hand must remain as far away from the patient as possible with the palm facing down and pointing to the floor. When the therapist perceives that the energy has flowed from the diseased area through his or her body and has reached the positive hand, he or she has finished their work and should wash their hands immediately in order to cleanse themselves of any impurity.

The other operation, that of infusing vital energy into the body of the patient, is performed in reverse, that is, by placing the positive hand on the area of the body that the healer wishes to heal while keeping the negative hand up high, with its palm facing up, receiving the energy that will be transmitted to the patient. This infusion technique may be carried out with the healer behind the patient, placing his or her hands on the patient's head, and visualizing a powerful white light penetrating the body of the patient and cleansing him or her of any disease.

Psi Healing

Psi healing, also known as shamanic, paranormal, or psychic healing, as well as bioenergotherapy, refers to the practice of fighting disease without the intervention of a known therapeutic agent.

These healing methods are considered paranormal precisely because they don't have a medical explanation at this time. Psi healing, one of so many modalities of alternative medicine, dates back to the dawn of civilization. We have already mentioned psi healing, in the same form as it is known today, being practiced in the Egyptian temples of Isis, Osiris, Busiris, and others. It is known that the Egyptian architect Imhotep, the high priest of Heliopolis, was the physician to all pharaohs up to the time of his death, which took place around the year 3000 B.C. Hippocrates, father of modern medicine, thought that a healing vital force existed, the *vis medica-*

trix naturae, and he would often lay his hands on his patients in order to heal them.

Of course all those who practice psi healing don't have the same explanation for this phenomenon. Some attribute the healing power to God, while others think that the cures take place through the intervention of universal energy, and yet many others believe that this therapeutic practice is based on the body's own repair mechanism, since mental power can strengthen the immune system and restore health. This last variant has been tried with undeniable success with many cancer patients who were trained to visualize the white blood cells of their immune system destroying invading cancer cells, one by one, until remission of the disease was successfully achieved.

Psi healing is performed most often by the laying of the hands, as practiced by Mesmer and also as explained by Carlos Castaneda in his book *Magical Passes: The Practical Wisdom of the Shamans of Ancient Mexico* (HarperCollins, 1998), in which he expounded on the keys to energetic conditioning. Thanks to the teachings he learned from the *naguales* Juan Matus and Julián Osorio, Castaneda gained access to the knowledge that each of us has an inherent amount of energy, which may not be increased or decreased but does need to be redistributed within the body when it falls ill in order to foster and initiate internal harmony, the basic principle of bodily health. As explained by Castaneda, Mexican shamans are able to perceive the flow of energy when they reach an altered state of consciousness which he called increased awareness. Through magical passes, shamans establish a desired connection between the energy guidelines of their bodies and the vibrating flow of universal energy.

Naomi Hintze, in her book *The Psychic Realm: What Can You Believe?* (Random House, 1975), reports the case of Colonel Oskar Estebany, who in the course of his military career realized that it was possible to heal by the laying-on of his hands. When Col. Estebany's fame reached Franciscan nun Justa Smith of Rosary Hill College in Buffalo, she decided to carry out her own research to see whether he was indeed able to influence cellular enzymatic activity. The results were satisfactory. Later on the colonel submitted to other investigations performed by Dolores Krieger of New York University, in order to find out whether indeed Estebany successfully healed by the laying-on of his hands. Dr. Krieger ascertained there were noticeable increases in hemoglobin levels in the patients who received his treatment.

Next you'll find some meditations intended to increase the healing power of your hands. You may use any meditation to which you feel particularly attracted.

The Sphere of Energy

If you find yourself unexpectedly in a situation in which a person needs healing, you should find a place where you can be isolated for a while.

Close your eyes. Relax.

Visualize a sphere consisting of a transparent material that surrounds you.

Think that only positive, health-enhancing energies can enter this sphere.

Imagine that all of this energy contained in the sphere starts to enter your body, and that from that moment on you can project that energy through your hands to the person you want to heal.

Open your eyes, feeling that you hold the power of healing in your own hands.

Healing and Cosmic Consciousness

Close your eyes.

Breathe deeply and slowly.

Return to your natural breathing.

Imagine you fly to outer space, soaring over cities, mountains, and rivers until you leave behind the planet on which we live.

Keep on traveling through space among the stars.

As you go on traveling, stretch out your hands to establish communication with Cosmic Consciousness. Ask this Consciousness for the power to heal, while promising that you will never use it for your own self-interest.

Return by doing the same journey in reverse. See that the Cosmic Consciousness is inside of you, ready to flow through your hands to serve others.

Healing Hands

While you meditate, join both palms with the same devotion as if you were praying.

Start to rub your hands slowly.

Imagine the universal energy coming to your hands as you rub them.

Try to visualize this energy. See how it sparkles and shines through the tips of your fingers.

Think that now you have healing hands, capable of providing health to anyone that needs it.

Self-Healing Exercises

Any of the meditations you chose to enhance the healing power of your hands may and should be combined with some kind of self-healing exercise. These tension-relaxation exercises will enable you to release pent-up tension. In addition, since the hands play an important role in the mind-body connection, they can direct the power of consciousness to the deepest cellular layers, where bodily health resides.

Exercise 1

Choose a quiet room, free of all noise.

Lie on your back. Close your eyes.

Tighten up your upper back muscles. Then relax them.

Now tighten up your shoulder muscles. Then relax them.

Tighten up the muscles of your arms, forearms, and hands. Then relax them.

Now tighten up, at the same time, the muscles of your shoulders, arms, forearms, and hands, stretching and tensing up the fingers of both hands as much as possible.

Relax. Enjoy the pleasant sensation brought on by relaxation, which will enable you to experience a higher level of energy and peace of mind.

Exercise 2

Sitting comfortably, stretch your right hand with its palm facing up.

Tighten up its muscles as much as possible, keeping the stretched fingers apart.

Without slacking off the tension, flex your thumb toward the base of each finger, starting with the little finger.

Now have each finger get as close as possible to the base of the thumb, first the little finger and then the rest.

Relax your hand. Draw your hand near your face, caress your face, and have your hand descend down your body, caressing your chest, your belly, your hips, and your thighs, intending your right hand to infuse with health.

Do the same thing with your left hand.

Exercise 3

Sit comfortably. Close your eyes.

Stretch both hands with their palms up. Tighten them up, keeping your fingers as separated as possible.

Imagine that each fingertip is being transfixed by healing energy.

Now keep up the intention that energy is accumulating in your hands, penetrating your whole body and flowing through all your organs, revitalizing them.

Relax your hands while pronouncing the word "health" mentally, with the same evoking power of a mantra.

Once you open your eyes, thank the universal energy for the benefit it granted you.

Exercise 4

Sit comfortably, with your eyes closed, take a deep breath and let the air out as slowly as possible, while lifting your hands, keeping the palms of your hands facing forward as when a person is asked to lift his or her hands while threatened with a gun.

Now tighten your fingers as much as possible. While you keep taking deep breaths, prolonging more each time the period preceding exhalation, fingers should be bent toward the palms, while keeping them tightened up. Feel the tension going up from the wrist to the forearm.

Relax. Lower your hands slowly. Repeat several times the word "health" in a soft voice.

Part VII

Zen and Self-Realization

We ought not to practice a selfish Zazen,
but rather a universal Zazen,
jointly with the whole Cosmos.
It is useless to try to save only oneself.

—Taisen Deshimaru

We should start by asking what is Zen, but no one has been able to provide an appropriate answer. No Zen master has attempted to define it categorically. There may be, in fact, as many versions of Zen as people who have practiced it. One of the great Chinese Zen masters, Hui Neng, who lived in the seventh century, always refused to explain to his disciples the methods to achieve enlightenment since, as of that very moment, Zen would become for the disciple a knowledge acquired instead of a personal experience.

"Zen masters," said Suzuki, "neither deny nor affirm." On another occasion he stressed: "Zen does not teach, it points out." Zen is not a religion since it does not worship any god or has anything to do whatsoever with an afterlife. It is not a philosophical system either. Perhaps, without much pretension, we could define it as a method intended to strengthen the mind-body relationship, whose highest objective is satori, that is, self-realization. So we have to look for Zen inside each individual. Zen is the appropriate way to get in touch with the most intimate forces of our inner being. The aim of Zen is to give man control over his own self. It taps the inborn goodness of man. It aims to bring out all the virtues that dwell inside human beings and expose these virtues to the light.

All of these objectives are pursued in and obtained through *Zazen*. Zazen means "sitting down in a lotus position while devoted to profound meditation." In Sanskrit it is equivalent to *Dhyana*, which literally means to "direct the spirit toward something." Dhyana, therefore, aims to focus the spirit on a certain objective, exactly the same thing we do when we practice meditation.

In Zazen all provisions must be carefully observed, as expressed first by Buddha and later on by Bodhidharma, who in the sixth century introduced Buddhism to China. From China, Buddhism found its way to Japan six hundred years later. When performing Zazen it is advised to sit in front of a wall, in a room where the utmost silence prevails. Throughout the whole process of meditation several incense sticks should be burned in order to induce a feeling of purity that will foster the mind-body relationship. It is preferable to perform two meditation sessions daily, one in the morning, before breakfast, and the other in the evening, before going to bed. The first sessions may last five to ten minutes. After two or three months they should be extended to thirty minutes. The meditator should assume the lotus position. When Tibetans meditate, they place their right hand, which represents discipline, over their left hand, representing wisdom.

In Zen it is the reverse. In reality there are five categories of Zen, with slight variations in the way they recommend the crossing of the legs or the placement of the hands, but they all have elements in common: the back upright, controlling one's breath and mental concentration. There is a Zen called *Bompu*, practiced solely for the purpose of improving health. Another Zen, called *Gedo*, is performed to acquire paranormal faculties. The third category of Zen is called *Shojo*, which means "small vehicle" or *Hinayana*, because its only purpose is to achieve peace of mind, whereas the aim of the fourth category, *Daijo*, "large vehicle," or *Mahayana*, is man's inner self, his most inaccessible zones. The fifth category, *Saijojo* Zen, is its highest form: absolute liberation, the one practiced by Shakya-muni Buda under the tree until he had achieved enlightenment.

Mind Control

After assuming the appropriate posture, the following step in the Zazen consists of controlling the breathing rhythm, counting the inhalations and exhalations in order to foster concentration. The next step in Zazen could be focusing on the breathing rhythm only with the "mind's eye" until reaching the so-called "awareness of breathing," which leads us to perceive clearly the mind-body rela-tionship. However, meditation's ultimate purpose is not exactly to follow the breathing rhythm with our mind in a state of absolute quiet.

Zazen, as we should understand it, is not inaction but quite the opposite. It implies a devotion to control one's mind for the pur-pose of using it with zeal and energy in order to achieve the most supreme objective: the transformation of the meditator into a new being, perhaps the new man Saint Paul talked about—a man with a fully developed mind, with all of his creative faculties at his disposal. Buddha preached that all sentient beings were able to achieve en-lightenment immediately, here and now. You don't need to wait until later, until tomorrow, or for an afterlife.

Obviously anyone can acquire the formula—it suffices to medi-tate with the firm determination of attaining true freedom. Without any ritual or intercession by any divinity, by simply following the dictates of the inner self, the individual can become self-actualized. Expressed like that, it seems an easy task, but it is not so easy be-cause it requires a great deal of willpower. "Even if I am only left with skin, sinew, and bones, and even if my flesh and my blood dry away and wither, I shall never move from this seat until I reach full enlightenment," it is reported that Buddha said when he set out to meditate under a tree where he remained sitting for the span of six years until he attained his goal. An identical feat was performed by Bodhidharma, who sat for nine years in front of a wall until he achieved spiritual actualization.

Whether achieved easily or through a sustained effort lasting many years, enlightenment is within the reach of anyone who pursues enlightenment with perseverance. It is within our reach for a very simple reason: all the conditions required for full self-actualization already exist inside each of us. We only have to believe that we are all potential Buddhas, accepting without arrogance that since birth we are programmed to reach the same state of awareness attained by Buddha and Bodhidharma. That is why Buddhism teaches that any fortuitous event, which supposedly has no special transcendence, may cause in a person his opening to satori, to spiritual actualization. Something apparently as insignificant as the falling of a fruit from a tree, the unexpected flight of a butterfly, or the light of dawn may be the trigger to the discovery of a new world, of peace of mind, and an inner joy that had been denied to us by the hasty rhythm of modern life.

Have you ever felt overwhelmed by happiness without knowing why? The memory of a particular moment of your life when you were totally happy comes back to make you smile years later? Have you felt the same emotion you experienced months or years before in the company of a loved one? Why do you feel like walking in the rain? A biochemist might explain that during those moments we are synthesizing endorphins, a hormone of the encephalin family that has a direct relationship with the feelings of happiness and physical well-being. Even if this scientific interpretation were true (and it is), at the same time elsewhere, during those very moments in which we are temporarily much happier than others, we are receiving intimations of the higher state that awaits us—fleeting flashes of the enlightenment that we can reach by meditating, through which mirth, happiness, and physical well-being will achieve permanence and become treasures that no one will be able to steal from us.

Any Technique Is the Best

Of all the meditation techniques described here, you can choose whichever one you like best, the first that exerts some kind of special fascination over you. The technique that will serve best your purposes of self-actualization is the one in which you place greater trust, the technique you put your faith in, because it is not the technique but rather you yourself that guarantees the result. It is not the technique that cures an illness but rather cellular intelligence responding to the requirements of a technique. What activates the organism's repair system is the confidence one places upon oneself when one sits down to meditate.

The technique should not be dismissed, however, because underneath that technique, supporting it, there are centuries of experimentation and results. We all know that just as one action is the result of all actions that have preceded it, knowledge is the sum total of all the knowledge that has been acquired throughout history. Persevering in the performance of a technique that has already been made sacred by the practice of thousands of people, including the founders of the great religions, is the best of all options.

These techniques have opened the channels that lead directly to self-actualization. We do not disregard, for example, the results obtained when we assume the position or perform the gestures that are appropriate for the practice of Zazen.

If we place our hands in *gassho*, that is, putting the palms together, we are immediately taken over by a sense of reverence and humility. If we place our hands on our lap and put together the tips of thumbs we feel peace and serenity, whereas if we sit with our back upright we experience a feeling of dignity.

The technique teaches us to decipher the wisdom of the body. The body's gestures are controlled through the practice of meditation until we perceive a close relationship, for example, between the fingers and the brain. The ancients were aware of this relationship. Anaxagoras said; "Man can think because he has a hand," and Taisen Deshimaru in his comments on the Sutra of the Great Compassion added: "We should learn to think with our fingers."

The Face of God

Possibly it is not us but God who chooses the moment of our enlightenment. Hindus say something similar when they say that the Master appears when the disciple is ready to receive him. God awakens to the life of the spirit only those who have earned the merits to be granted that grace. In the eyes of God, merit, according to all religions, resides in the practice of virtues such as compassion, loving our neighbor, and altruism. Merit also resides in the discipline, dedication, and will power we invest in and for the sake of our spiritual enhancement. If no effort is invested, no advancement will be attained, as in "no pain, no gain." Without a yearning for perfection aimed at the highest purpose, which is enlightenment, it will not be possible to achieve this goal.

Zen is not entertainment at the disposal of the person next door who has nothing to do. It is instead an uphill path with no return that must be climbed as you would a flight of stairs—step by step. At the end, watching us from the highest point, is the face of God. It is precisely there, at the highest point, that the encounter with ourselves takes place. Each person, when he or she gets to contemplate the face of God, observes his or her own face. God's image is, perhaps, the synthesis of the faces of all beings that inhabit the universe.

Meditation paves the way to this encounter with our "inner me." In the course of this encounter we see the first hints of the Light. But when we finally reach enlightenment, that instant which in a certain way marks the culmination of our life, we see for ourselves that it does not exactly coincide with our physical death. The Upanishad says that after enlightenment a man can "leave behind his body and rest forever in the Brahman's bosom or, on the contrary, preserve his body's integrity."

The soul is free from that moment but the person continues to live. As of that unique experience, the enlightened lead a paradoxical life, since even though they continue to live among us, sharing our happiness and difficulties, in some way they belong to another world: they are controlled by attachments, live in perfect harmony with themselves, and all their actions are aimed at fulfilling a higher purpose that keeps them permanently in touch with cosmic wisdom. They are the scholars, the great literary and artistic creators, the scientists who through their discoveries and research are blazing new paths to understanding.

After enlightenment it is common that they may live for a very long time. Buddha lived for forty-five years after achieving his own. We should not be surprised, therefore, that anywhere, at a movie theater, a library, at the waiting room of an airport, we come across an enlightened being, that is, with a person who achieved wisdom, who escaped from the traps constantly laid by vanity, selfishness, and absence of love. Mozart was an enlightened being. So were Tolstoy and Goethe, as were Shakespeare, Gandhi, and Martin Luther King Jr. However, it is not necessary to distinguish by fame. We may discover in a person, who may be our next-door neighbor, the indecipherable, yet simultaneously revealing signs that the enlightened bear on their foreheads. Lida, my guardian angel, was also enlightened and yet she went through life quietly, without making any noise, without showing off her infinite merits and knowledge, her boundless wisdom, lavishing her love on others without asking anything in return.

To attain enlightenment, we can follow any of the five Zen categories, but whatever path we take must be paved with love—love for ourselves and love for others. If you don't rejoice over others' success and happiness, you won't be able to love yourself. Without love there is no health, physical beauty, or spiritual richness.

Allow the alchemy of love to transform each beat of your heart. into pure gold

Self-Actualization and Success

Based on the law expounded by Hermes Trismegistus, i.e., "That which is above is the same as that which is below," we can say that self-actualization is a concept that does not only involve our spiritual growth—it also defines our attitude toward life and the results we manage to garner in society. Therefore self-actualization may be the same, in a certain way, as something we all seek: success.

Success may be defined as the result of the ability or skill used to reach the most desired goals with minimum effort. Contrary to the belief of many, the happy achievement of an aim does not result primarily from the tenacity shown by the individual, that is, from his or her stubborn determination to beat their head against the wall, fall back in defeat and get on their feet again. If we analyze carefully the true laws that govern success, we'll see that these laws involve acquiring a state of internal harmony that allows all the abundance contained in the universe to flow to the successful individual rather than hard work, sacrifice, and self-denial.

Paramahansa Yogananda wrote *The Law of Success: Using the Power of Spirit to Create Health, Prosperity, and Happiness* (Self-Realization Fellowship, 1981). Recently Deepak Chopra and other authors have broached this subject, and they all concur in affirming that one of the main spiritual laws of success is the law that reminds us constantly that inside ourselves we have all these potentialities which, being latent, are just waiting for the right moment to express themselves physically and be transformed from pure energy into visible and palpable matter. All of this potential becoming a reality for us, overwhelming us with happiness, health, and financial gain, depends almost exclusively on our mental attitude, so getting programmed for success is not a matter of just wishing and working arduously to achieve an objective, but rather allowing the mind to attract the object of our desires by tapping the great reserves of creative imagination.

Many people equate success with abundance of material things. Having money may be an indication, but countless other people, without material riches, have satisfied their expectations and fulfilled their own lives certain of having achieved successfully the goals they set out for themselves. It suffices to mention the most obvious names: Jesus Christ and Buddha. Unfortunately it seems that most people don't make use of their abilities to attain what they desire, but rather quite the contrary: they are constantly putting obstacles in the way of their own self-development with a broad array of negative attitudes, ranging from pessimism and skepticism to lack of self-confidence and fear of the changes life holds in store for us. The mechanisms that most frequently lead to failure are frustration, loneliness, resentment, aggressiveness, and uncertainty. Each of these negative tendencies were created by people who suffered them at some point in their lives, presumably in their childhood or adolescence, as a means to solve a problem or back away from a painful situation. And since they continue programming our behavior in our subconscious, these tendencies surface when we face a situation similar to the one that made us feel inferior, afraid, or helpless for the first time.

What we should try to do, then, is to program for success instead of failure, guided by a mental attitude that will lead us smoothly to success. "Most individuals are as happy as they want to be," said Abraham Lincoln, which is to say that if we want to place that positive programming at our service and to our advantage, we should start by knowing the mind's mechanisms.

In his book *On Vital Reserves, the Energies of Men: the Gospel of Relaxation* (Holt, 1911), the psychologist William James recommended to avoid brooding constantly about vexing problems and their hypothetical consequences. To get rid of these worries, anxieties, or fear of failure, of all those ghosts that inhabit the subconscious, the most effective method, according to James, is to substitute passivity for activity, and relaxation of stress for the intensity of our ideas. This method, which he called the *surrender technique*, advises us to concern and involve ourselves with a certain issue only until the moment we decide to carry it out and indeed carry it out. As of that very moment, if we want to maintain our mental health and promote the achievement of our goals, we ought to quit thinking about the consequences of our actions, leaving the solution of these issues in the hands of higher forces, perhaps in the hands of a Higher Being able to lead our aims and desires to a happy conclusion.

These higher forces which William James mentioned are not only outside of us, but also inside, that is, in the Microcosmos, in our inner self, and we only need to learn to harness them and place them at our disposal by storing in the subconscious the greatest number of possible positive ideas that we need to achieve success. Making use of these inner forces to create short-term or long-term goals for ourselves, and seeing these goals come true on the physical plane within the desired time-span is not so difficult or complex as one might suspect. We simply have to have complete confidence in the results we are going to get, which will depend certainly on our ability to meditate while visualizing these goals in absolute detail, as if we have already accomplished them. If, for example, you wish to get a good job, buy a home, or achieve marital happiness, you only need to place yourself mentally in the desired situation as if it were already part of your reality. Your energy and your mind will then achieve your objectives.

Love, Astrology, and Meditation

Three thousand years before the birth of Christ, the first Persian priests who were initiated in the knowledge and practice of astrology divided the heavens into four equal parts: Taurus' Aldebaran, Pisces' Fomalhaut, Scorpio's Antares, and Leo's Regulus. Later on the Sumerians subdivided these four parts and thus we ended up with the twelve zodiac signs as we have them today. Under each sign the stars and the planets exert a very specific influence on the various aspects of our personal life—health, home relationships, latent abilities, social status, and, of course, also on love.

At the exact moment of our birth, or perhaps before, at the moment of conception, when the unicellular egg is fertilized, we become recipients of astral influences, we establish the first relationships of the Microcosmos with the Macrocosmos and start to synchronize our biological clock with the rhythms of universal energy. According to many scholars of occult sciences, as soon as the head of the newborn emerges from the mother's womb, it is the pineal gland or the Chakra of the Thousand Petals that captures those first astral outflows, which will remain forever in our internal universe, inside each one of our cells, in our nervous, hormonal and immune systems. These outflows will be coded, in this life and in our future successive lives (if we accept the theory of reincarnation) in a DNA molecule, which not only contains our genetic potential but is also one of the points where the information of our cosmic lineage is stored. Such astral outflows, which very early on turn into our own flesh and blood, will permanently dictate our inclinations, preferences, desires, aptitudes, and feelings.

Who can question the characterological accuracy that astrology attributes to each solar sign? Who can doubt today that a person has tendencies to exercise authority, perhaps excessively, precisely because he or she was born under the sign of Leo? How can we question the influence of the stars when it has been possible to prove that a person's blood conditions are closely related to solar radiations? Doesn't science teach us that depressive states known as "seasonal affective disorder" are suffered by certain people in the winter, specifically because during this season of the year the blood carries high levels of melatonin, the hormone secreted by the pineal gland? It has also been proved that night crimes are not most frequent on the darkest nights, but quite the contrary, on the nights with a full moon, when the moon is at its brightest.

Dante Alighiere finished his *Divine Comedy* with this verse: "love, which moves the sun and the stars." If in astrological terms we can say that love is a feeling conditioned by the date, hour, and place of our birth, we can also say in poetic terms, like Dante, that our love, the love we give our mate, the love that dignifies sex and turns two twin souls into a single being, also exerts a beneficial influence at a cosmic scale by making our life on this planet more pleasant and beautiful. But how can we know who is our twin soul? How can we discover that soul among the huge crowd that fills the streets of the large cities? How to discover that we can establish such a gratifying relationship with that person? How to detect it? Are there astral influences that promote our marital happiness? Can we consult the stars to choose our mate?

Everything indicates that the answer is yes.

Aries, which governs the head, is the first sign of the zodiac. Since it is a sign of Fire, Arians should have a satisfactory love relationship with those born under a Fire sign: Gemini, Libra, and Aquarius. Between Arians and those born under Taurus there are evident irreconcilable differences. However, in the area of love they can sustain excellent relations, especially if the mate born under

Aries is the male, who feels a strong attraction to the capacity for sexual enjoyment of the woman born under Taurus.

Taurus is an Earth sign; that is why its natives get along with those born under a Water sign: Cancer, Scorpio, and Pisces.

Natives of **Gemini**, an Air sign, feel attracted to those born under a sign of Fire: Aries, Leo, and Sagittarius.

Natives of **Cancer**, a Water sign, are destined to have a satisfactory love relationship with natives of Earth: Taurus, Virgo, and Capricorn. Cancer-Cancer relations are very promising in terms of mutual understanding.

Leo, a Fire sign, will have a gratifying relationship with natives of Libra, Gemini, and Aquarius, which are all Air signs.

Those born under **Virgo**, an Earth sign, can sustain enduring relationships with natives of Cancer, Scorpio, and Pisces. Virgo and Capricorn natives usually tend to have long-lasting relationships.

Astrology has come to call **Libra** natives "Peacemakers" because of their innate capacity to keep their internal balance, which allows them to establish, at least hypothetically, a pleasant and almost always long-lasting relationship with those born under any other solar sign.

Scorpio, which governs the sex organs, is a Water sign that gets along well with Taurus, Virgo, and Capricorn, which are all Earth signs.

Sagittarians may have excellent love relationships with natives of Gemini, Libra, and Aquarius, whereas:

Capricorn natives get along with those born under Cancer, Scorpio, and Pisces. The Capricorn-Capricorn relationship is also auspicious for happiness.

The reason **Aquarius** (the Water Carrier) is an Air Sign and not a Water Sign is a mystery. Aquarius relates harmoniously with Fire Signs: Aries, Leo, and Sagittarius.

Finally, natives of **Pisces**, a Water Sign, have promising and enduring love relationships with those born under Earth Signs: Taurus, Virgo, and Capricorn.

Love is a mutual feeling. True love is born with a surprising spontaneity, most often as two future lovers exchange glances for the first time. Suddenly they become aware, without needing an explanation, that they were born for each other. When someone experiences true love, that person establishes a communication and a bond with the person for whom that love is intended. This first communication, not yet put in words, a sudden impulse from the heart, is represented symbolically by Cupid's mythical arrow. Cupid is never wrong, and soon the twin souls, who had intuitively been seeking each other, are joined on the physical plane.

Through meditation it is possible to strengthen this initial bond, to the point that love flows harmoniously between both, and there is nothing or anyone who can be in the way. To perform these meditations the elements belonging to each zodiac sign should be taken into account, as we said before.

The Houses of the Zodiac

Here is an example: you want your love relationship to flow in perfect harmony to a person born under a Fire sign. Here are the steps to follow:

1. Close your eyes. Relax.

2. Visualize in as much detail as possible the person you have chosen.

3. Now imagine a flame that's just started. It may be a bonfire in the forest, or the small flame on a lighter, whichever you prefer.

4. The flame is your love energy. Get it closer to the object of your love.

   See the flame shine around that person, illuminating her (or his) figure, providing her (or him) with a warm and pleasurable sensation.

   See that person smile gratefully.

5. While the flame is still alive, illuminating the scene, you must wish the best for that person, confess how much you love them, express how much you want to make them happy.

6. When you finish your meditation, before opening your eyes, repeat mentally, as many times as you can or as you wish to, the word "love."

If the person chosen is a native of an Earth Sign, in the course of the meditation you must visualize that person lying on her or his back on the earth, perhaps in the midst of fruit-bearing trees, the way Eden must have been. You must tell that person that the earth that supports her is like the love you feel. Swear that you will always give her the same protection and stability that the earth on which that person lies provides her.

If that person is a native of an Air Sign, tell that person in the course of the meditation that the air that you have visualized for her (or for him) that is now caressing her face so pleasantly is the energy of your love. Promise you'll always provide her with the same feeling of happiness and well-being she is experiencing now, thanks to your meditation.

If the person was born under a Water Sign, tell her (or him) in the course of your meditation about that water, that liquid element you have visualized for their enjoyment, so they can delightedly dive and splash in a pool or a beach, the water symbolizing the happiness with which you will always provide them.

How to Awaken Latent Abilities

A prominent Russian hypnotist, Vladimir Raikov, who worked for several years at the Moscow Psychoneurological Clinic, did not use hypnosis to heal the sick, as most of his colleagues did, but rather to help people bring forth their latent talents and abilities. How did Raikov achieve this? By using hypnosis to induce in a person the character or talent of another in order to enhance his or her own faculties.

Under a hypnotic trance the person is induced to believe that he or she is a famous writer, painter, or singer. Raikov said: "When the person comes out of the trance, he or she can keep the abilities of the person that was suggested."

Raikov was enthusiastically referring to the cases of numerous individuals who never studied painting or attended any art school or even touched a brush, who after hypnosis turned into professional painters, with expositions that earned favorable reviews in the newspapers and magazines of his country. If Raikov told a person under hypnosis that he or she was Leonardo da Vinci or Albert Einstein, that person would unquestionably come to believe it at a subconscious level and later on could even become a great painter or eminent physicist.

The explanation offered by Raikov is the following: during childhood we all have a great many talents, but as we grow older and our mind develops, we start to distribute our mental abilities, strengthening some while rendering others null. Hypnosis releases those innate faculties, so it is possible, as Raikov asserted, that there is a clear connection between hypnosis and creative genius. Raikov also thought it possible that a person under hypnosis, since in that state he or she is not limited by the notions of time and space, could project him- or herself into the future and bring back the knowledge achieved by humanity fifty or a hundred years later.

Perhaps that sort of foresight was the achievement of the famous American clairvoyant Andrew Jackson Davis, born in 1826 in Poughkeepsie, New York. Davis' clairvoyant powers were awakened by a hypnotic session performed by a hypnotist in his hometown. Davis performed medical diagnosis under a hypnotic trance, and was even able to read and see with his eyes closed. According to Arthur Conan Doyle, in his book *The History of Spiritualism* (Arno Press, 1975), among Davis' best-known predictions were the internal combustion engine and the typewriter.

Another prominent American clairvoyant was Edgar Cayce, who was called "the sleeping prophet." Cayce would articulate his prophesies and his accurate medical diagnoses by harnessing the powers of meditation. It is said he would close his eyes as if he were sleeping, and he would start to talk. When he would wake up, perhaps half an hour later, he could not recall what he had said but he had foretold events that would come true with astonishing accuracy, such as when he prophesied that England would lose control of India. Long before psychosomatic medicine became a subject of conversation, Edgar Cayce had already explained that stress caused gastric ulcers, and that most diseases originate in the mind due to frustrations, resentments, or anger. His diagnoses of diseases in people he had never seen were also extraordinarily accurate. Equally surprising were his cures at a distance, even in cases in which conventional treatments had failed. Some of Cayce's healing methods are similar to those currently used by hypnotherapists. Cayce said: "If the ideas delivered to the subconscious are good, the body improves."

Man becomes self-actualized when he attains spiritual enlightenment. That's the moment he reaches the summit of human evolution. Kundalini, the powerful energy center within us, right at the base of the spine, has moved up through all the chakras and levels of awareness and starts to shine at the very center of the head, providing all of the splendor of the Chakra of the Thousand Petals, from where it then establishes a fluid exchange of information with the Cosmic Intelligence. This is the process that turned Siddhartha Gautama into the Buddha. It's the same spiritual transformation that awakens all the latent abilities in a human being, turning him into a saint or a genius.

Reaching enlightenment means going beyond all limitations, but before a person may begin to enjoy this transcendental event, he or she can project him- or herself into the future, as Davis and Cayce did, or succeed in actualizing many of their hidden abilities by using a method similar to the one used by Raikov in hypnosis. To achieve these objectives, the following positive affirmations should be stated in the course of meditation:

1. I am wisdom.

2. I am full of optimism.

3. Life is a source of knowledge for me.

4. My latent abilities emerge at this moment.

5. I'll put my talent at the service of others.

6. I have within me the necessary power to strengthen my will and organize my daily activities.

7. I have the necessary capacity to successfully carry out all my projects.

How to Materialize Money

Since everything is energy, so is money. A dollar bill is nothing but crystallized energy, something that was in our mind and finally materialized. This type of materialization was called precipitation by Master Kuthumi, and in a certain way he defined it as the process whereby a thing, an object, passed from the ethereal plane to the physical one, which is the same as to say that nothing exists if no one has imagined it previously, if no one made it come true with his thoughts in our measurable and palpable world.

If we make money by publishing a novel, that's because the characters in that literary work first dwelled in our imagination, and because before the novel was printed those characters talked and moved in the confines of our mind, exactly the way an oil painting existed in the painter's imagination before coming to life on the canvas. No money will get into our pockets unless our energy, whether it be physical or mental, takes part to foster the occurrence of this event.

Do you know the various ways to mobilize energy to get money? Some might be as unusual as the following.

After assuming the meditation position, think of one or several drawers. Visualize them full of money. Think of all the money you need or want, and put it in the drawers. Once you complete the visualization do not perform another meditation about money or drawers, because you run the risk of imagining it differently and interfering with the development of the original design.

Result: the money will come to you, perhaps in the manner you least expected, and also within a shorter time span than you thought. A piece of advice: don't waste money because money is like air: if you open all of the doors and windows of your house, money will leave as easily as it came. Don't hoard it away either, the way misers do, because money is like water—if it stagnates, it loses its energetic momentum and stops being useful to its owner, as well as to others.

With a smile, a friend told me of her experience that was the result of an immovable conviction: in the course of a meditation she mentally filled all her drawers with all the money she wanted, and that same week she received the news of a large inheritance from a relative she hardly remembered. Facts like these seem to lead into fanaticism and superstition, but they are all well documented and unquestionably confirm that for mental power there are no impossibles.

Master Kuthumi said that the only difference between an Ascended Master and an individual who has not awakened, i.e., who has not achieved enlightenment, is the quality of feelings and thoughts. "Each of us has the same creative powers, the same free will, the same energy and the same extraordinary ability to mold that energy." Since science and mysticism have started to shake hands, quantum physics supports Master Kuthumi's same point of view. Heisenberg's Uncertainty Principle assumes that at a sub-atomic level "we cannot observe anything without affecting it." The observer and the observed are constantly interacting. Or what amounts to the same thing: there is no independent observer who can observe without transforming the observed object.

Sai Baba is an avatar, that is, a divine incarnation currently living in India. On numerous occasions, in front of hundreds of people who come to meet him, Sai Baba raises his hand and materializes in the air any object: a ring, a medal, or other item, and hands it over as a gift to one of those present. One day a journalist asked him: "Do you believe you are God?" Sai Baba replied: "Yes, and so are you. The only difference between us is that you don't know."

Part VIII

Seven Healing Meditations

1.

Go into a room where you can remain in total silence. Be seated—a chair, a sofa, a cushion, whichever you like best. Close your eyes. You will start to feel a state of relaxation spreading throughout your body. At first it won't be easy, but think of the muscles of each part of your body and see how they relax. For example, when you think of your chest muscles repeat mentally: "All my chest muscles are loose, at ease, relaxed; loose, at ease, relaxed; loose, at ease, relaxed." Repeat this three times on each area of your body. You will see that you are taken over progressively by a pleasant sensation.

Extend your arms over your thighs, with the palms of your hands facing up. Feel how energy comes to your palms. Experience the presence of energy as a sensation of heat or a tingling on your palms. Now raise your hands little by little. Start getting them close to each other, so the palms are face to face.

Appreciate the energy circulating between the two palms. Perhaps you may be able to visualize this energy as a ball of light between your hands. Caress this ball of light, noticing its texture. Now separate your hands and become aware that energy grows as your hands become separated. You may also realize that energy is now elastic and therefore has stretched and grown between your hands.

Start playing with energy as a child would with a toy. Shape it. Start making figures with this energy: trees, doves, stars, whatever you like.

Now you are ready to add these figures to your body. Allow the figures to "jump" from your hands and enter your body through the skin. They may enter through an orifice high up on your head.

Fill yourself with these figures. You have become a vessel where these figures (clear glass-like trees, doves made of pure air, stars consisting of liquid crystal—figures into which you have molded your energy) are going to be stored. Fill your whole body with these figures, from head to toe. Now open your eyes and thank universal energy for the sense of well-being it has given you.

2.

Breathe deeply and slowly. Imagine that you are inside the House of Health. A guru greets you ceremoniously by putting his hands together at his chin and slightly bowing his head. Sit on a soft cushion of freshly cut grass. Assume any position: the lotus position or any position that makes you feel comfortable. Keep your back straight and start focusing on your breathing rhythm. Breathe in. Breathe out. Prolong the pauses between inhalation and exhalation, without strain or fatigue.

There is a fountain in front of you that you had not seen before, which just turned up as if by magic. Water does not spring from this fountain but rather in spurts of blue light that go up and down. Although it is light, the spurts go up and down as if they were water, just like any other fountain in a park. Now the spurts reach higher, the fountain grows, its limits expand and are getting slowly closer to you, until the light envelopes you completely.

Now you are sitting inside the fountain of blue light. The streams of light color your skin. You have become a blue person from head to toe. You can half-open your eyes and see for yourself. Your hands and forearms are blue. Look at them. Your legs, your whole body has taken on a fascinating blue color. Keep focusing on your breathing rhythm and see the light penetrating you through your nostrils, invading your whole body, painting it blue. Review in your mind your whole body within, your head, your thoracic cavity, your abdomen, your hips, your thighs, your legs, and your feet. Everything is incredibly, beautifully blue within.

Feel the happiness afforded you by being blue. Enjoy this unique pleasure, this unexpected joy. Only when you deem it necessary, the Fountain of Blue Light will return to the place and size it occupied previously and finally disappear.

You may now stand up, say good-bye to the guru by putting your hands in gassho if you so desire, thank him for the benefits received, and temporarily leave the House of Health, with the promise of returning to it whenever you so need.

3.

Relax. Breathe deeply and slowly. Think of a beautiful fish, such as one you may have seen in a fish bowl, perhaps an iridescent fish that swims slowly through the water. Stop and observe the movement of its tail and gills. This fish has a name: it is Healer Number One.

Someone who never deceived me once told me that if you ask this fish, it is able to fight a pain or a disease you might be suffering. Observe the fish reach the affected area and start to suck away the pain or the disease. Trust its restoring function.

There are other fish, which also have names: Healer Number Two, Healer Number Three, Healer Number Four, Healer Number Five, and Healer Number Six, who are willing to work for your health. If you get to observe them, see how each of these healing fish take away pain or disease from your body.

Before opening your eyes, thank any of them, or all six, for the service they have just rendered you.

4.

Try to attain a pleasant state of relaxation by breathing deeply and slowly. Close your eyes. Imagine that you stand up, leave your house, walk down several streets in your city, and get to a place full of trees.

Already inside this forest, stop walking and for a while focus all your attention on the chirping of the birds and rustle of the wind as it goes through the branches of the trees. Some of the trees are big and luxuriant, others have a thin trunk and scant foliage. Suddenly one of the trees becomes particularly attractive to you. In your imagination separate it from the other trees and watch it intently. Experience the sensation that between this tree and you there is a connection, first of kinship and then of love.

You must start to think that you love this tree as you would a son, your mate, or your parents. In an instant start loving it as much as you love yourself, because suddenly you have also realized that you have entered the tree, because somehow you've become aware that the tree is yourself, because your arms have become transformed into the branches of the tree and your body into its trunk.

Imagine that your feet are the tree roots and that these roots penetrate deep into the earth, from which they extract the nourishment needed in order for the tree to be full of energy and the branches to become fully green.

Imagine firmly that you are that immense tree and start to breathe within it, feeling that all the energy of the universe penetrates your body through the branches and the leaves of the tree that is you.

When you find it convenient, leave the tree and the forest and return home, walking back down the same street until you arrive back in the room where you are sitting. Now open your eyes slowly and start to stretch as if you awakened from a restful sleep.

5.

Close your eyes. Relax.

Breathe deeply and slowly as many times as you can without becoming tired or fatigued.

Return to your normal respiration.

Visualize in the distance a huge soap bubble with a beautiful blue color.

The bubble rests on the line of the horizon and, although it is at quite some distance, you start walking toward it very slowly, even though you are sure that very soon you will be next to it.

Now that you have it at hand, think that you must remain inside of it for some time.

Enter the bubble. Imagine that you are safe from any concern or disease, that a pleasant sensation of peace and well-being takes you over.

While you focus completely on your breathing rhythm, you should start to think that all of your body (your skin and organs) takes on the same blue transparent quality as the bubble.

Think that when the meditation is over and you abandon the bubble, happiness and well-being will remain inside of you for as long as you desire.

6.

In a state of relaxation visualize a sponge. Have it grow in your imagination to the point you can fit inside the sponge.

Think (because visualizing is thinking) that the sponge is soaked with water.

Visualize that you enter the sponge. Remain inside for as long as possible, imagining that the water runs throughout your whole body, flowing slowly inside of you, from your toes to your head.

Imagine a huge hand (which could be God's hand), a hand ten or twenty times as large as your own. Imagine that this hand get close to the sponge, takes it away from your body and your home, and then squeezes it.

Imagine that the water extracted from the sponge has taken away all the impurities that used to be in your body. Now think that your body has become clean and pure from within. Think of this intently.

7.

Now you are going to meditate inside this book. This book is a long meditation. If you are sitting comfortably and breathe deeply and slowly as advised, it will be possible for you to enter these pages very easily, go over them one by one, and realize that they contain all the Masters that have been mentioned—Jesus, Buddha, Lao-Tzu, Bhodhidharma, and many, many more.

There are Masters on all the pages, sitting in the lotus position, meditating. There are gurus advising on the need to meditate, the way to benefit our bodies through the practice of meditation, and the ways to reach enlightenment. Now you too sit to meditate on a page. That page is yours—it was intended for you. Every time you want you can return to it, sit down and meditate.

It doesn't matter that you are under the impression of having turned into a tiny figure, sitting in the lotus position on a page of this book. As your size is apparently smaller, spiritual height will be inversely higher.

Have you realized, without arrogance, that by meditating inside the book you are the same as the Masters?

Have you realized that by just setting out to achieve this goal with persistence, enlightenment can be attained?

Bibliography

Alvarez López, José. *El Hatha Yoga y la ciencia moderna.* Editorial Kier, Buenos Aires, Argentina, 1959.

Blay, Antonio. *Energía personal.* Ediciones Índigo, Barcelona, España, 1990.

Bloomfield, Harold. *Meditación Transcendental.* Ediciones Grijalbo, Barcelona, España, 1975. Original title: *Transcendental Meditation.*

Cleary, Thomas. *Antología Zen.* Editorial EDAF, Madrid, España, 1993. Original title: *Zen Antics.* Shambhala Publications, 1993.

Cousins, Norman. *Anatomía de una enfermedad.* Editorial Kairós, Barcelona, España, 1979. Original title: *Anatomy of an Illness.* Bantam Books, Inc., 1981.

Devi, Indra. *Yoga para todos.* Editorial Diana, Buenos Aires, Argentina, 1959. Original title: *Yoga for Americans.* Prentice Hall, 1959.

Hirsig, Huguette. *Astrología médica.* Editorial Printer Latinoamericana, Colombia, 1994. Original title: *L'Astrologie Médicale.*

Jung, Carl. *El secreto de la flor de oro.* Editorial Paidos, Buenos Aires, Argentina, 1955. Original title *en alemán: Das Geheimnis Der Goldenen Blüte.*

Kieffer, Gene. *Kundalini para la Nueva Era.* Editorial EDAF, Madrid, España, 1989. Original title: *Kundalini for the New Age.* Bantam Books, 1988.

Lévi, Eliphas. *Dogma y ritual de la alta magia.* Editorial Humanitas, Barcelona, España, 1991.

Mehl-Madrona, Lewis. *Medicina Coyote*. Editorial Grijalbo, México, 1998. Original title: *Coyote Medicine*. Simon & Schuster, 1998.

Merton, Thomas. *Meditaciones sobre Oriente*. Ediciones Oniro, Barcelona, España, 1997. Original title: *Thoughts on the East*. New Directions Publishing Corp, 1995.

Sachs, Robert. *Ayurveda Tibetano*. Ediciones Obelisco, Barcelona, España, 1994. Original title: *Health for Life, Secrets of Tibetan Ayurveda*. Clear Light Publishers, 1995.

Saddhatissa, H. *Introducción al budismo*. Alianza Editorial, 1971. Original title: *The Buddha's Way*. George Brazillers Publishers, 1972.

Shapiro, Debbie. *Cuerpo-Mente*. Editorial Printer Latinoamericana, Bogotá, Colombia, 1990. Original title: *The Bodymind Workbook*. Element Books, 1992.

Su Santidad el Dalai Lama. *La fuerza del budismo*. Ediciones B, S.A., 1996. Original title: *La force du Bouddhisme*.

Suzuji, Daisetz Teitaro. *Introducción al Budismo Zen*. Ediciones Mensajero, Bilbao, España, 1986. Original title: *Die Gross Befreiung*.

Varenne, Jean. *El Yoga y la tradición hindú*. Plaza & Janes Editores, Barcelona, España, 1975. Original title: *Le Yoga*.

Weil, Andrew. *La curación espontánea*. Vantage Español, New York, 1997. Original title: *Spontaneous Healing*. Ballantine Books, 1996.

Other titles of

Smriti Books

ANCIENT TEACHINGS FOR SPIRITUAL GROWTH
(Written by Douglas De Long)

Ancient Teachings for Spiritual Growth is designed to let you fully develop your psychic abilities in a surprisingly short time. Revealed in these pages are the original teachings of the Enlightened Masters: Jesus, Buddha, and Zoroaster, and the secret wisdon of the Egyptian and Atlantean temples. By uncovering and distilling the essential teachings and practices of the ancient mystery schools, Douglas De long has created a step-by-step lesson plan that will allow you to quickly activate your latent inner powers. Learn to: Open the *chakras* • Read the aura • Contact the spirit guides • Project the astral body and • Delve into past lives.

250 pages, 140 x 215 mm **ISBN : 81-87967-68-4**

Rights: **Indian Subcontinent**

GOD MEN CON MEN
(Written by Robert Carr)

This dazzling book is written straight from the heart. It is the story of a 'lonely' American who has always lived on the edge. In this book Robert rewinds and replays with heartbreaking simplicity the emotional memories of his lifelong struggle to find out the meaning and the mystery of life. I would call him a 21st century Siddhartha.

344 pages, 140 x 215 mm **ISBN : 81-87967-58-7**

Rights: **World**

SPIRITUAL MASTERS: SAI BABA
(Written by Sonavi Desai)

Sai Baba of Shirdi is one of the most well-known spiritual Masters of India. He belongs to that brotherhood of saints who crossed the barriers of caste and creed and spoke the universal language of love. He taught the most profound philosophy and the greatest truths in a simple and forthright way.

This book is a collection of stories, portrayed through the eyes of Laxmi, one of his closest devotees. While material facts have been kept intact, an element of fiction has been introduced to weave events from his life into a narrative. This book hopes to encourage the reader to reflect on Baba's teachings and inspire a desire to understand the timeless wisdom passed on through our yesterdays.

179 pages, 140 x 215 mm **ISBN : 81-87967-63-3**

Rights: **World**

SPIRITUAL MASTERS: THE BUDDHA
(Written by Supriya Rai)

The Buddha, Siddhartha Gautama, lived and taught over 2500 years ago. His teachings comprised some of the highest moral philosophy then known to man and appealed to the rational and the poetic mind alike. He led a remarkable life, travelling and teaching ceaselessly for 45 years after attaining Enlightenment. Today, Buddhism is one of the world's most widely practised religions, drawing followers from lands far away from that of his birth. In this book, three men narrate the story of the Buddha's life. One is his son and disciple, Rahula. Another is King Bimbisara's charioteer, Triguna, who is a creature of fiction. The third narrator is Ananda, a cousin and disciple of the Master and later, his attendant. As they proceed with the narration, their understanding of the Master's Teaching deepens, enabling each one to achieve his own transformation.

154 pages, 140 x 215 mm ISBN : 81-87967-64-1

Rights: **World**

TREASURES OF BUDDHISM
(Written by Frithjof Schuon)

Far from discounting the providential "mythology" of the person of the Buddha, the author relates its historical—and sometimes contradictory—phenomena to its celestial roots in the Divine Qualities and to the human virtues that form the necessary framework for spiritual life. Notions crucial to Buddhism such as suffering and its cessation, void-form, nirvana-samsara are elucidated in the light of the Vedantic distinction of Atma-Maya, providing an important key to understanding the differences between Western philosophical "individualism" and the serenity of Eastern metaphysics.

216 pages, 140 x 215 mm ISBN : 81-87967-57-0

Rights: **Indian Subcontinent**

THE CIRCLE OF KARMA
(Written by Joshua Mack)

What is Karma, exactly? Is it punishment? Payback through divine intervention? A universal method of checks and balances? Karma is really none of that. *The Circle of Karma* sets out to explain the fundamentals. From the initial recognition of Karma and the Buddhist perspective to the western world's adoption of Karma, the author brings it out of antiquity and strips it down to its essence, so that you understand it in the context of your everyday life. Featuring a mixture of amusing anecdotes, compelling lessons, and solid instruction, this book:
* Defines Karma in a straightforward manner
* Debunks the myths surrounding Karma
* Suggests ways to apply Karma to your life.

158 pages, 140 x 215 mm ISBN : 81-87967-66-8

Rights: **Indian Subcontinent**